Countdown to Non-Fiction Writing

Countdown to Non-Fiction Writing provides all the support you need in helping pupils to improve their non-fiction writing. It is a comprehensive and flexible resource that you can use in different ways, and includes:

- 37 stand-alone modules that cover all aspects of writing and understanding non-fiction texts, including the nature of language, logical thinking, recognising 'facts' and planning;
- A countdown flowchart providing an overview showing how modules are linked and allowing teachers and pupils to track their progress;
- Photocopiable activity sheets for each module that show how to make decisions and solve problems that writers face on the journey to a finished piece of work;
- Teacher's notes for each module, with tips and guidance, including how modules can be used in the classroom, links to other modules and curriculum links, and advice on helping and guiding pupils in their writing;
- A self-study component so that pupils can make their own progress through the material. This option gives young writers a sense of independence in thinking about their work and, through offering a scaffolding of tasks, encourages confident and effective writing;
- 'Headers' for each module showing where along the 'countdown path' you are at that point.

In short, *Countdown to Non-Fiction Writing* saves valuable planning time and gives you all the flexibility you need in helping pupils to prepare for, understand and write non-fiction. The structure of the book allows teachers to utilise the modules for 'self-study', as a longer programme following the 'countdown' structure, or to dip into the book for individual lesson activities and ideas to fit in with wider programmes of study.

Additional online resources to support this text are available at www.routledge.com/9780415492591

A former teacher, **Steve Bowkett** is now a full-time writer, storyteller, educational consultant and hypnotherapist. He is the author of more than forty books, including *Jumpstart! Creativity* and *A Handbook of Creative Learning Activities.*

Countdown series

Steve Bowkett

Developing pupils' writing abilities boosts their confidence, creates enjoyment and relevance in the task and cultivates a range of decision-making and problem-solving skills that can then be applied across the curriculum. The Countdown series provides all the support you need in helping pupils to improve their prose, poetry and non-fiction writing.

Also available

Countdown to Creative Writing
978–0–415–46855–8

Countdown to Poetry Writing
978–0–415–47752–9

Countdown to Non-Fiction Writing

Step by step approach to writing techniques for 7–12 years

Steve Bowkett

Routledge
Taylor & Francis Group
LONDON AND NEW YORK

First published 2010
by Routledge
2 Park Square, Milton Park, Abingdon, Oxon OX14 4RN

Simultaneously published in the USA and Canada
by Routledge
270 Madison Avenue, New York, NY 10016

Routledge is an imprint of the Taylor & Francis Group, an informa business

Typeset in Frutiger and Sassoon Primary by
Florence Production Ltd, Stoodleigh, Devon
Printed and bound in Great Britain by
MPG Books Group

British Library Cataloguing in Publication Data
A catalogue record for this book is available from the British Library

Library of Congress Cataloging in Publication Data
Bowkett, Stephen
Countdown to non-fiction writing: step by step approach to writing
techniques for 7–12 years/Steve Bowkett.
p. cm.
Includes bibliographical references.
1. English language – Composition and exercises – Study and
teaching (Elementary). 2. English language – Composition and
exercises – Study and teaching (Middle school). 3. Creative writing –
Study and teaching. I. Title.
LB1576.B5363 2010
372.62′3 – dc22 2009016668

ISBN10: 0–415–49259–9 (pbk)
ISBN10: 0–203–86741–6 (ebk)

ISBN13: 978–0–415–49259–1 (pbk)
ISBN13: 978–0–203–86741–9 (ebk)

Contents

Introduction

The well-known science fiction writer, Theodore Sturgeon (1918–1985), is remembered among other things for coining three 'laws'. The first is that *nothing is always absolutely so*. The second and most famous asserts that *90 per cent of everything is crap*. And, just in case you were curious about it, Sturgeon's third law is *it is not possible to assemble a device with small parts without dropping one in a deep-pile carpet*. You may be relieved to know that I will concentrate more on the first and second laws and have very little to say about the third.

It seems to me that the concept of non-fiction is fraught with difficulties. At its most basic level, anything that purports to be 'non-fictional' consists of ideas that must have passed through at least one human mind. And as we all know, humans blend thoughts and feelings together in an endless variety of ways, creating outcomes that are a rich mixture of facts, opinions, other distortions, deletions and generalisations. In other words, creating a unique interpretation of some aspect of the world forged into complex patterns of language. Added to that, we have to contend with the extra complication that once something is read or heard it is *reinterpreted* by the reader/listener so that its meaning fits more comfortably with that person's 'map of reality' – with his or her individual network of memories, beliefs, intentions and so on. A teacher of mine always prefaced his lectures by saying 'I am responsible for what I say, but not for what you hear'. Perhaps this is what Sturgeon had in mind when he suggested that 'nothing is absolutely so'. Is a fact still a fact if it is wrapped up in an opinion? How can we ever really check for ourselves the veracity of a fact or determine its truth? Can something still be true if it is not a fact? How could we decide if something was clearly not a fact? What do we mean when we use the word 'true'? Are the words 'real' and 'true' interchangeable? Is non-fiction always true?

These sound rather like philosophical questions, which is something else this book touches upon – given that I'm defining philosophy here simply as an exploration of words and their meanings within the context of deciding what counts as non-fiction. And if that sounds as though it might be a little 'heavy', I'll try to make sure it's not. Encouraging children to engage in philosophical enquiry can be great fun and in recent years has grown into a movement that has flourished in many British schools. I was delighted to find it happening in one I visited not long ago. I enthused to a Y5 boy 'Oh great, so you do philosophy in this school!', to which he replied 'Well, it depends what you mean by "philosophy" and "school." And "you".' I knew then that the programme was working well.

I want to lay my cards on the table early on and state that my main intention in this book is not just to help children write non-fiction clearly and effectively. I'm more concerned with showing them how to use the mental tools that might give them a better chance of recognising (if we accept Sturgeon's figures) the 10 per cent of everything that is not crap. And I am not being frivolous. The most influential educational book I have ever read is called *Teaching as a Subversive Activity*, written by Neil Postman and Charles Weingartner (see Bibliography). I still have my college copy on the bookshelf and refer to it often. In this uplifting and deeply angry book you will find chapter headings such as 'Crap detecting', 'What's worth knowing?', 'Pursuing relevance' and 'Meaning making'. The authors assert early on that one of the primary aims of all schools should be to supply every pupil with a fully functional, robust and constantly evolving crap detector, and in *Countdown to Non-Fiction Writing* I have taken my cue from them.

The fact is (if I can get away with saying that) we live in not only an information-rich world but one where language is power, as it has always been: or more precisely we might say that the ability to influence others through language is power. So the deeper agenda I have in mind is about raising children's awareness of how language can influence, so that they do not become unwitting victims of its power, together with offering them strategies for using words more influentially themselves. In aiming for these goals we'll be looking in some depth at creativity and thinking skills, which form the underpinning of the writing the children produce. A further educational benefit for us (and for them of course) is that the 'creative attitude' and the more critically incisive thinking they learn to do can be applied directly to all other areas of the curriculum. In other words, this is not simply a book about one aspect of literacy but it has broader ramifications that ultimately reach beyond the children's school lives and indeed beyond childhood itself.

Like the other books in the *Countdown* series, this one consists of a series of modules that progress through a sequence to the 'Blastoff' point, where (it's my intention) children will be able to write more capably than they could at the outset. Each module includes pupil pages containing various thinking/discussing/writing activities, and many also feature teacher's notes suggesting extensions to those activities, links to other modules, further references and resources and so on. The modules are more or less self-contained and so can also be used individually with particular pupils to focus on a specific topic or task, or can be built into your own programmes of work.

Most importantly, in using the modules with the children I urge you to 'model the attitude' that forms the ethos of the book. In another important work (*Overschooled but Undereducated*; see Bibliography), John Abbot makes the point that younger children's learning is 'clone-like'. They learn largely by imitation, and can develop some pretty sophisticated skills that way. In the context of learning about non-fiction the attitude might be described as 'question, doubt, challenge', which, when combined with the willingness to engage in playful curiosity and the urge to find out more, will never harden into a limiting cynicism. My only fear is that you'll succeed with the children so well that they'll apply Sturgeon's second law to the pages that follow . . .

See overleaf for the *Countdown* flowchart.

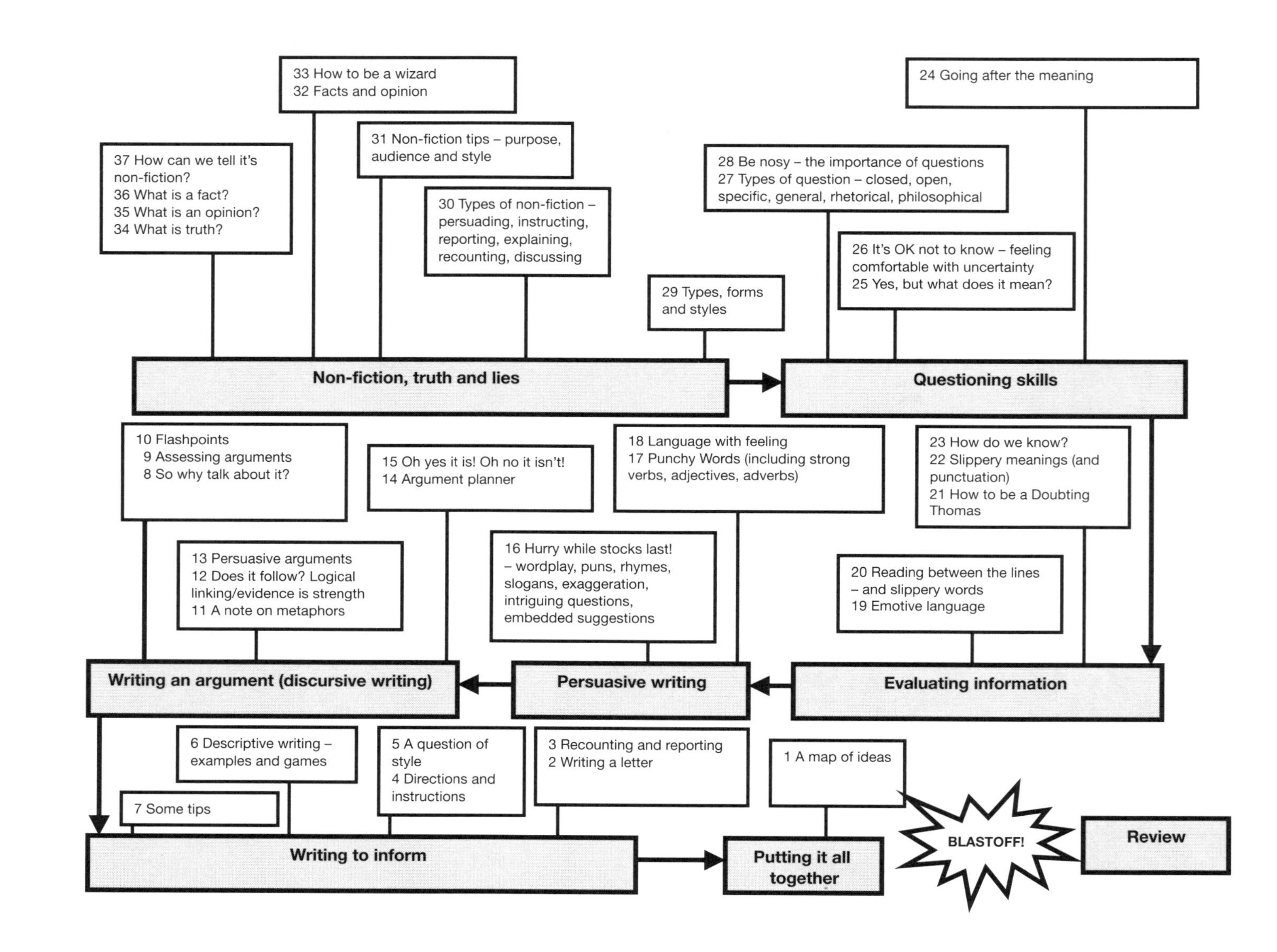
33 How to be a wizard
32 Facts and opinion
24 Going after the meaning
37 How can we tell it's non-fiction?
36 What is a fact?
35 What is an opinion?
34 What is truth?
31 Non-fiction tips – purpose, audience and style
30 Types of non-fiction – persuading, instructing, reporting, explaining, recounting, discussing
29 Types, forms and styles
28 Be nosy – the importance of questions
27 Types of question – closed, open, specific, general, rhetorical, philosophical
26 It's OK not to know – feeling comfortable with uncertainty
25 Yes, but what does it mean?
Non-fiction, truth and lies
Questioning skills
10 Flashpoints
9 Assessing arguments
8 So why talk about it?
15 Oh yes it is! Oh no it isn't!
14 Argument planner
18 Language with feeling
17 Punchy Words (including strong verbs, adjectives, adverbs)
23 How do we know?
22 Slippery meanings (and punctuation)
21 How to be a Doubting Thomas
13 Persuasive arguments
12 Does it follow? Logical linking/evidence is strength
11 A note on metaphors
16 Hurry while stocks last! – wordplay, puns, rhymes, slogans, exaggeration, intriguing questions, embedded suggestions
20 Reading between the lines – and slippery words
19 Emotive language
Writing an argument (discursive writing)
Persuasive writing
Evaluating information
6 Descriptive writing – examples and games
5 A question of style
4 Directions and instructions
3 Recounting and reporting
2 Writing a letter
1 A map of ideas
7 Some tips
Writing to inform
Putting it all together
BLASTOFF!
Review

FOR THE TEACHER

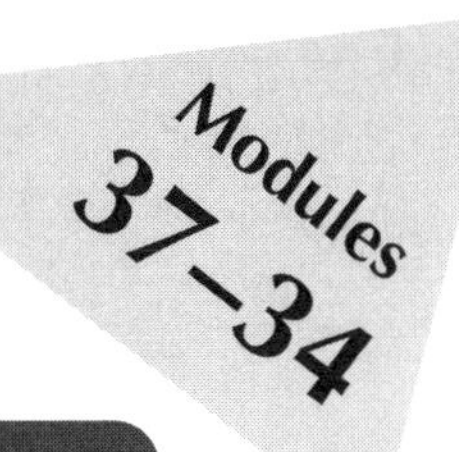

Section 1 Non-fiction, truth and lies

Fiction or non-fiction, truth or lies?

A useful starting point in helping pupils to attempt to answer the questions in these modules is to discuss with them what might be called the 'relevant vocabulary' of non-fiction. I have often come across children (and plenty of adults) who use words without any clear idea of (1) what *they* mean by them and (2) what the words mean in a wider context, including their etymological roots. If we accept the notion that 'I am responsible for what I say but not for what you hear', then it is always worth checking the speaker's/writer's intended definitions – as far as this is possible – or at least stating clearly the meaning that one has put upon a particular word or term.

One of my most-thumbed reference books is a little dictionary of word origins I keep on my desk. Over the years I have got into the habit not just of investigating particular words I want to use but also browsing in a more leisurely way. Building ten minutes' browsing time occasionally into your classroom routine is bound to produce some interesting results. The children are likely to enjoy it too and, very importantly, they might well develop the habit of saying 'Yes, but what do you mean by that?' I grant that this could be annoying from a teacher's point of view, but it's a cause for celebration, I think, that the children are developing the 'question, doubt, challenge' attitude.

As an example of what I mean, I was intrigued to learn that 'fiction' has its origins in the Latin *fictio*, the 'act of fashioning', from *fingere* 'to shape or feign', which in turn has links with the origins of the word 'dough'. This threw up a number of useful insights for me.

Modules 37–34

FOR THE TEACHER

The notion of deliberately fashioning language and meanings 'like dough' is a very kinaesthetic idea that tactile learners especially can 'get to grips with'. Concrete metaphors are likely to be remembered more surely than abstract definitions.

The word 'feign' means to invent and to forge, this word itself having associations of shaping and of deceiving – to forge a signature or a banknote and so on. So deeply implicit in the word 'fiction' are the notions of 'making up' and 'deception'. But what do we make, then, of fables and parables, which can be profoundly true? This opens up an interesting topic of discussion with the children that can encompass other relevant words in our enquiry.

A further implication is that non-fiction must be what fiction is not, which clearly isn't always the case. The whole notion of 'spin' in politics and the media belies the idea that factual material 'means what it says on the tin'. Discussing with children the question 'When is a fact not a fact?' will undoubtedly lead to further insights about the hidden agendas that often underpin the presentation of factual ideas and their supposed links with 'the truth'.

Other words that you might consider exploring with your class are: fact, lie, opinion, authentic, authority, expert, truth, exaggeration, embellishment . . . I'm sure you can think of many more.

Another important aspect of engaging with non-fiction is that of relevance.* Relevant arguments, for example, are not just logically valid or sound but often make an emotional appeal to the reader and/or are aimed at a specific audience. For our particular purposes it's worth raising children's awareness of relevance with regard to the kinds of non-fiction writing they will be asked to do, where 'sticking to the point' counts for a lot, as does the personal-emotional relevance of what's being said. More on this as we count down towards Blastoff.

(* The word comes from the Latin 'to raise up' but also has links with 'lever' and the Latin word *levis* – 'light in weight'. How might these insights be used to help children understand the rather abstract notion of relevance in their non-fiction writing?)

How can we tell it's non-fiction?

Hello and welcome to our countdown towards writing non-fiction. Your teacher will probably have explained how this book works but, if not, let me mention that the modules in here are mainly about the way you *think* and also how thoughts can affect the way you feel. Words express your thoughts and feelings, of course, but what other people say and write can influence how you think and feel. Maybe your teacher will ask you to look at certain modules in a certain order, or perhaps you are allowed to choose for yourself. Either way, I hope you'll enjoy the journey and learn some useful things.

Activity: Writing non-fiction

So we've got together here to find out more about writing non-fiction. Before we go any further I'd like you to do two things:

1. Write a sentence telling us what you think 'non-fiction' is. If someone has already explained it, will you put that into your own words please?
2. Make a list of how you know that a piece of writing actually *is* non-fiction. What clues do you look for to help you decide?

Here are some of the ideas other children have given me.

I know it's non-fiction because . . .

- it's not made up. It's true;
- non-fiction contains facts;
- non-fiction teaches you things and helps you to learn. For example, a book about science is non-fiction;
- non-fiction isn't like a story because it doesn't have a plot or characters. And it's not like a poem because it doesn't rhyme (or other things that poems do!);
- Non-fiction takes a certain *form*, like a letter or a recipe or an essay.

What do you think about those ideas? You are allowed to disagree with them as well as agree. You can also add to any of them if you want to.

Activity: *Questions about non-fiction*

We're not quite finished yet. When I was working with the class that had these ideas, I asked them then to think of questions they might ask about the definitions they'd given. Work by yourself or with friends and do the same – what questions can you ask about the bulleted list above? Some of ours follow below:

- What about stories that have real facts in them – are they a mixture of fiction and non-fiction?
- Can a poem about, say, learning your nine-times-table be called non-fiction?
- What is a 'fact'?
- If a fact is approximate, is it still a fact? Is an exact answer a 'better' fact?
- If a professor said 'In my opinion such-and-such is true', does that count as a fact?

If you want to, you might even discuss one or two of your questions or those above in class – or maybe suggest to your teacher that you'd prefer a longer playtime instead.

Now choose another module in this block – **What is a fact?** (**Module 36**), **What is an opinion?** (**Module 35**) or **What is truth?** (**Module 34**).

What is a fact?

Do you have an answer to that question already? If so, mention it to your teacher and classmates now. I think this is a very important point, because much of your time at school is intended to be spent learning facts. A dictionary will tell you that a fact is something 'certainly known to have occurred or be true' and also that it reveals 'the realities of a situation'.

Activity: Facts

That sounds quite straightforward, and so we learn that facts are connected with knowledge, certainty, truth and reality. But are things always as simple as that? Take a look at these statements . . .

1. Pluto is the ninth planet in the solar system.
2. I got out of bed this morning.
3. Edward VII is the King of the United Kingdom.
4. A rose by any other name would smell as sweet.
5. The Earth is round.

If a fact is supposed to be something known, certain, true and real – which of these are facts? Actually it doesn't matter if you don't know, because my next question is – how can we find out which of the statements are facts? Make a list of ways we can try and find out, then compare your ideas with mine:

- I can ask an expert, or several different people.
- I can look it up (in a book, on the Internet etc.).
- I can work it out for myself.
- I can go and see for myself.

Of course, I can't try all of these in every case! Your ideas and mine are about ways of checking (or *verifying*) that a fact is in fact a fact – if that makes sense!? So what about statements 1–5 above? Which ways would you choose to verify them as facts? Whether you try and verify them or not, what are your thoughts about them? Here's what I reckon.

1 Pluto was called a planet until very recently, but then it was termed a 'plutoid' (sounds a bit rude to me). Now I think it's called a 'dwarf planet'. People are still arguing about it. Some people want to call it a 'minor planet' and some want to call it a 'trans-Neptunian object' (an object beyond the planet Neptune). We could reasonably ask – does what something is called alter the reality or truth of it? Pluto is still Pluto, whatever it's called.

2 The only way you can check this is by asking me (or my wife or my cat). Although you might use your own *experience* and *reasoning* to decide it's a fact. You might say 'Well most people go to bed at night, and for Steve to have written that statement he probably got up in the morning.' So we can say the statement is quite likely a fact, but when all is said and done it's a pretty boring one! Or, to put it another way, the fact is not very *relevant*.

3 Have you heard the expression 'the devil is in the detail'? Sometimes a small detail or error can make a lot of difference. The statement is not a fact, although if it said 'King Edward VII *was once* the King of the United Kingdom' it would be – or so the history books tell us. We learn here that checking carefully is important when verifying facts.

4 William Shakespeare said that (in his play *Romeo and Juliet*, Act 2, Scene 2, lines 40–41). You can check that for yourself. But what about the statement itself – is it a fact or an opinion? And would it be Shakespeare's opinion or Juliet's?

5 This is an interesting one, I think. First, we have the problem of what we mean by 'round'. A coin is round, so is that the right word or the best word to use? We could say 'the Earth is a sphere'. That brings us closer to the truth. But geographers know that the Earth is flattened a bit at the poles and bulges a bit at the equator. They call that shape an *oblate spheroid* – what a mouthful (and messy to say when you're eating biscuits). So here we learn that some facts are not absolutely accurate, but are close enough to the truth to serve our practical everyday purposes. But sometimes we need to be exact in our facts, and that might mean getting technical.

Time now to jump to another module – I suggest **What is an opinion?** (**Module 35**) or **What is truth?** (**Module 34**). Before you go, you might want to check with your teacher where the word 'fact' comes from. You might be surprised . . .

FOR THE PUPIL

What is an opinion?

The word 'opinion' comes from old Latin words meaning 'to think, judge, suppose and choose'. To have an opinion is to make a judgement or hold a belief based on something less than proof – and *proof* comes from Latin too, from words that mean 'to test and approve' and 'that which is good and honest'. Perhaps we can say then that the best/strongest/most useful facts are those that have been tested and proved?

Activity: Opinions

But what about opinions? Here are some questions for you to think about and discuss:

- What opinions do you hold strongly? How did you come to have them?
- If you hold an opinion strongly, does that mean you must have strong feelings about it?
- Should an opinion be based on facts? If an opinion is not based on facts, but on strong feelings instead, is it just as convincing (to you?).
- How could we decide if someone's opinion is worth having ourselves?
- If someone has an opinion, but can't explain any reason for having it, is that opinion worth anything? In other words, if I said 'Strawberries are the best fruit' and you said 'Why?' and I said 'Well, just because', would my opinion carry any weight?
- Look at these statements and decide which one is true:
  - A rose by any other name would smell as sweet.
  - A rose by any other name would not smell as sweet.

OK, I'll confess: I tried to trick you with that last one. Read what I asked you to do once more. Notice that the way I said it is trying to make you think that one of them *must* be true (and that therefore the other one is false). But it would be perfectly reasonable to say 'Well it depends on various things.' Your judgement would be even stronger if you could name some of those things.

Maybe you'll agree with me that people often feel strongly about their beliefs and opinions (is an opinion a belief, by the way?). Also, it's often the case that people try to convince others that their opinions are 'right' – but be careful of that word. I'll say more about it later. Finally, you can of course have any opinions that you like, but the more reasons and facts you have to back them up, the stronger I think they will be.

In my opinion you should go to **What is truth?** (**Module 34**). Right now!

FOR THE PUPIL

What is truth?

They say that 'truth, like beauty, is in the eye of the beholder'. What do you think? But wait! – before you start thinking, let me admit that I'm trying to trick you again. Notice I began with 'they say', which is a commonly used phrase but actually is pretty meaningless. Who on Earth are 'they'? It's a *vague generalisation* and I'll have more to say about it later (for instance, in **Going after the meaning** (**Module 24**)).

Anyway, back to truth. The word itself comes from an Old English term meaning 'faithful' and before that from an even older language (Sanskrit) and a word that means 'tree' or 'wood'. I think that's really interesting. Why would the meaning of truth come from words about trees and wood? What do you reckon?

One thing most people seem to believe is that truth (whatever that means) is 'good' (whatever *that* means). Certainly as far as we are concerned, when we write non-fiction we want it to contain truth and not lies. So if I'm using facts in an argument I want to be as sure as I can that they are true and not made up. If I express opinions I want to know – and I want my readers to know – that they are based on reasons I think are true. If I write some instructions I want them to be accurate, which is another way of saying 'true' – or is it?

Activity: Truth

You can keep the idea of truth as simple as that if you want to. But if you'd like to explore a bit further then choose one of the ideas below to discuss:

- If you look in a dictionary, you'll see that truth is defined as something that is accurate, honest, sincere, factual. Do you think that these words mean the same thing? Are there any other words you could add to the list to talk about truth?
- Do you think that anything can be *absolutely* true? In other words, true on all occasions and under all circumstances? I'm thinking of something like 'The angles of a triangle always add up to 180 degrees' or 'It is wrong to deliberately take the life of another human being.' Are they always true, do you think (and why do you think it)?
- Here are some things various people have said about truth. Pick one of them and think about what it might mean. Decide if you agree or disagree with it (or how far you agree or disagree). Find out what some of your classmates think.
  - Believe those who are seeking the truth. Doubt those who find it. (André Gide)

- The truth is more important than the facts. (Frank Lloyd Wright)
- There are no whole truths. All truths are half-truths. (Alfred North Whitehead)
- Don't say 'I have found the truth' but rather 'I have found a truth.' (Kahlil Gibran)

By the way, one of my favourite quotes about truth is: *It is always the best policy to speak the truth – unless, of course, you are a very good liar*. That is from the writer Jerome K. Jerome.

There's a little bit more to say about facts and opinions in **How to be a wizard** (**Module 33**) and a couple of activities you can do if you want to (**Module 32**). Or you or your teacher might prefer to jump straight into looking at some common types of non-fiction at **Module 30**. Wherever you go – see you there!

Modules 33–32

FOR THE TEACHER

Fact, opinion and wisdom

Wisdom has its roots in Greek, from words meaning 'to see' and 'to know'. It is also related etymologically to the word 'wit', which has connotations of humour ('he's a real wit'), intelligence (being witty) and the senses ('keeping her wits about her'). Whether a wise person would agree with me or not is a moot point, but as far as I'm concerned the origins of the word 'wisdom' clarify a set of attributes that bed down into the kind of attitude I am aiming to cultivate in children in this book.

Vachel Lindsay's poem *The Leaden Eyed* (easy to find on the Internet) articulates the dark side of the point I'm making, that it is the duty of every adult to help ensure that children do not live dreamlessly and die 'like sheep'. I feel that one of the primary aims of education must be to develop:

- intelligence beyond the accumulation of facts;
- humour in the form of playfulness;
- the mental flexibility to look at things in many ways (including the ridiculous);
- 'the wits' in terms of observational skills and a sharpening of the other senses.

That endeavour, focused as it is here, will prevent children from becoming what we might call the passive victims of language and will enable them to use language as though it were a toolbox packed with diverse instruments.

We have begun to explore the fuzzy distinctions between fact and fiction, knowledge, belief and opinion through the approach of 'question, doubt, challenge'. As I've hinted above, this need not be done in an intense, academic or overly serious way. Some of the wisest people I've ever heard about (Albert Einstein, Freeman Dyson and Arthur C. Clarke to name a few) often took an almost childlike view of the world in terms of their overarching sense of wonder and fun, their sheer delight at exploring ideas, and their incisive ability to see 'beyond the given' (which is itself a powerful and useful definition of creativity). Modelling the attitude of people like this and making their ideas explicit will help enormously in encouraging children, as the old saying goes, 'not to follow in the footsteps of the wise, but to seek what they sought'.

FOR THE TEACHER

Practically speaking we can enable this by:

- Making displays of famous quotes and sayings.
- Changing one thing in your classroom every day and inviting children to notice what it is.
- Posing 'how come' questions often. How come the sun rises every morning? How come a liquid like petrol can make my car move? How come our bodies change all through our lives, but there's always the same sense of 'me' inside myself? How come bees know where to find the pollen in flowers?
- Asking 'what if' questions often. What if everyone woke up one morning and could no longer speak, read or write? What if our thoughts appeared in real thought bubbles over our heads? What if time travel was possible? What if I could meet any famous person from the past – what three questions would I ask?
- Looking for the wisdom in proverbs, parables, myths and visual symbols.

How to be a wizard

Did you know that the word 'wizard' originally meant a wise man (or, more fairly, a wise person)? In many myths and legends wizards or 'wyse men' used their power thoughtfully and were often great advisers to those who sought out their knowledge and experience.

I think it's important to realise that 'wisdom' can appear in both fiction and non-fiction writing. Myths, legends, fairytales and parables are fictional, but many of them contain really useful advice. If you don't think so, take a look at *Aesop's Fables*, for example, or some of the old Chinese tales you'll find here – www.101zenstories.com/.

Also, I believe it's true that facts and opinions can both *contain* wisdom and be *used* wisely (or unwisely of course!). Lots of proverbs and other kinds of sayings are wise. That is to say, they contain useful advice, shed light on problems and difficult situations, and suggest ways forward. Here are a few that I particularly like.

Proverbs:

- A stitch in time saves nine.
- Little strokes fell great oaks.
- As you sow, so shall you reap.
- Curses are like chickens, they come home to roost.
- Time is the best counsellor.

If you're not sure what these mean, chat with your teacher and friends. There could be several 'right answers' to each. In what ways do you think these proverbs are wise? Or if you don't think they are, why not?

Activity: Wisdom

Now find a few other proverbs that you feel contain wisdom, and be prepared to say why you think so.

Other wise sayings:

- Every good answer leads to more questions. (Anonymous)
- Out of clutter, find simplicity. In the middle of difficulty, find opportunity. (Albert Einstein)

FOR THE PUPIL

- A person who can't make a mistake can't make anything. (Abraham Lincoln)
- Life is a daring adventure, or it is nothing. (Helen Keller)
- All that glisters is not gold. (William Shakespeare) (See if you can find out what 'glisters' means.)
- When someone points at the moon the fool looks at the finger and the wise man looks at the moon. (Traditional Chinese saying)

Again, you might disagree that these contain wisdom. Whether you do or not, your view will be much stronger and more persuasive if you can say *why* you think so.

Notice how it's difficult to decide if proverbs and sayings like this are facts or opinions. What is clear (to me anyway) is that, when you want to write persuasively (see **Modules 18–16**) or construct a strong argument (**Modules 15–8**), they may be very helpful when used wisely and in the right place!

Now you can either test yourself by looking at some facts and opinions in **Module 32** or move straight on to explore different kinds of non-fiction writing in **Module 30**. But no need to rush; you know what they say – 'More haste, less speed'.

Facts and opinions

As I've already suggested, sometimes it's hard to decide whether a statement is a fact or an opinion. What about this? – Knowing your times tables by heart is often very useful. Is that a fact? Would you say that it is 'true'? What if we changed the sentence a little bit, would that change what you think about it . . .?

- Knowing your times tables by heart up to 12-times can often be very useful.
- Knowing your times tables by heart is always very useful.
- Most people would agree that knowing your times tables by heart is often very useful.

Do you see how things can get complicated quite quickly? Another point I want to make is that small or subtle changes like this can often affect the meaning of a statement quite a lot. The word 'subtle', by the way, means 'not obvious' or 'with fine differences'. Look again at the bullet points above. Can you think of any other ways of writing those sentences where, by adding or changing a word or two, you can change what the sentence might mean?

When you come to write your own pieces of non-fiction you are allowed to put opinions in – your own and other people's. But if you do you should *make it clear that it's an opinion*. You can say 'in my opinion . . .' or 'I think/feel/believe that . . .'. Or you can say 'according to Albert Einstein (or whoever)' or 'Albert Einstein believed that . . .'. Doing that is fair, open and honest.

As far as facts are concerned, when you put facts into your non-fiction the golden rule is to *be sure of them* (as far as you can be). In other words, check your facts as far as you can to make sure they're accurate. Sometimes this is hard to do, so the next best thing is to say where you got the fact from. You might say 'According to the *Encyclopedia Britannica* (or wherever)' – and then mention your fact.

Activity: Facts and opinions

Anyway, more on that later. Here are a few more statements. Are they facts or opinions? Could a statement be both? Can you spot any ways that the sentences are trying to trick you?

1 The planet Saturn has sixty moons.
2 In 1492 Christopher Columbus discovered America.
3 Milk is good for you.
4 The next sentence is a lie. The last sentence is the truth.

FOR THE PUPIL

OK, OK, I admit it – I'm trying to trick you *again*. If you questioned or doubted those four statements, then good for you. If you decided whether each was a fact or an opinion and said why you thought so, then good for you. If you said you didn't know if a statement was a fact or an opinion but thought about how you might find out . . . then good for you.

Here are the tricks I tried to play on you:

1 According to www.wiki.answers.com, Saturn has '60 confirmed moons since 2007'. So as far as we know it's a fact. But Saturn could have many other moons that we don't yet know about.

2 This is a *subtle* one – remember that word? In 1492 Christopher Columbus discovered a landmass that *later became known* as America. In 1492 'America' as such didn't exist. Some people call what I've just said 'nit-picking' or 'splitting hairs'. Can you find out why? What do you think? Is it splitting hairs or am I being careful to make sure that facts are accurate?

3 This is what's called a generalisation, or vague general statement. I imagine statements like this as clouds. They look solid enough, but you try and get hold of one! The word 'good' can mean all sorts of things. Apart from that, if a person is allergic to dairy products we couldn't say that milk was good for him or her. So the statement is a fact (or true) in some cases but not others.

4 This is a really slippery one! These two sentences make what is called a *paradox*, which is an impossible statement. Look again . . .

   (a) The next sentence is a lie. (b) The last sentence is the truth.

   If (a) is true then (b) must be a lie, which means that (a) is a lie. But that means (b) must be true, which means that (a) is true . . . You could go around in circles forever with that. Paradoxes are really frustrating, I think. You might not come across them often in your work, but they do show how sentences that seem simple at first glance can actually be fiendishly complicated.

   Another famous paradox is ' "All Martians are liars," said the Martian.' Can you work out why that is a paradox?

Anyway, now that you've pulled all your hair out, maybe you're tough enough to take a few more tips – go to **Module 31**. Or perhaps you want to take a look at the different kinds of non-fiction you might be asked to write. Set sail for **Module 30**. There's also the choice of **Module 29**, where you can learn about different forms and styles that the various text types can take.

Tips, types, forms and styles

It seems to me that the basic idea behind the differentiation of text types in the curriculum is to raise pupils' awareness of fitting style to purpose. An 'instructional' style would not therefore be expected to contain much – or any – persuasive/emotive language. On the other hand, reportage could legitimately feature opinion together with the straight transmission of facts, provided that these are clearly distinguished in the text: most usually in a newspaper article, for instance, more subjective commentary is inserted towards the end rather than in the earlier sections of the piece.

But be aware that the situation is much more complex than this. What kind of 'text type' is the paragraph you've just read for example? Ostensibly it's explanatory. If that's so, would you expect it to contain opinion or other kinds of subjectivity; or should my explanation confine itself to factual points? If the latter, how factual is the assertion that 'an instructional style would not be expected to contain . . . persuasive/emotive language'? It might be worth searching out some examples of instruction to test the idea.

With that in mind, one of my favourite Chinese recipe books, *Wok Cookery* is written by Don Slater (see Bibliography) and contains gems such as:

- The wok is easily the most versatile single cooking implement ever devised.
- Chinese noodles are foul when overcooked.
- Not least (this dish) will convince the most dedicated salad-maker that cooked cucumber is delicious.

Admittedly Don Slater tends to reserve these opinions for his introductions to recipes rather than putting them in the step-by-step 'how to' writing of the recipes themselves. But the point must be made that, if the interpretation and meaning of language are dependent upon its context, then at some point pupils must recognise that contexts are not always (or even often?) as simple and straightforward as they seem, or should be. In the case of *Wok Cookery* Slater's asides and personal commentaries give the book its individuality and add hugely to reader enjoyment – in my opinion.

The situation grows even more interesting when we look at newspapers and news media more generally. One of the basic lessons to learn is that the media are highly edited: information is selected, filtered, prioritised and presented with all kinds of hidden (or barely visible) agendas in mind. Of course, as mature savvy adults we know this. But how many children pass through the educational system without realising it? I feel that the more pupils are alert, aware and awake to bias, spin and hidden agendas, the more incisive will be their analysis of language contexts, and the more able they will be to weave language to suit their own purposes (bearing in mind that the root of the word *context* is 'to weave').

My agenda – not hidden I hope – in this book is to raise children's awareness of the way that language can manipulate, so helping to ensure that they do not 'die like sheep'. As teachers we can begin to do this early on in their education. A few hopefully practical suggestions you might consider are:

- Constantly encourage children to 'question, doubt, challenge'.
- Explore distinctions. What are the differences between explaining and instructing, for example? Or between reporting and recounting?
- Create a glossary of terms that can be used as 'tools' to raise awareness – bias, hidden agenda, spin, rhetoric, pattern-of-three, euphemism, generalisation and many others.
- Consider as part of your agenda the wisdom of the poet Matsuo Basho, who suggested that one can learn the rules well, and then bend them.

Non-fiction tips

As we saw earlier, even trying to decide if something is a fact or an opinion can be complicated. I think what's important is that you *look carefully* to try and work out what the writer is up to. Writers (or speakers) usually have reasons behind the language they use. Another word for reasons is 'purposes'. You should always ask 'What is the purpose behind this language'? Thinking about that will help you to understand two other important ideas – audience and style.

These three things are always connected:

- ▶ Style means the kind of language you're using.
- ▶ Purpose means the reason(s) behind the kind of language you're using.
- ▶ Audience means the people you're writing for.

These three things working together make up what is called the *context* of the language. The word 'context' (and 'text') means 'to weave' – a bit like the word textiles. Can you see how knowing that is helpful? In the same way that we weave cloth to make clothes of a certain style for particular people to wear, so we weave words and ideas to make language of a certain style for particular people to read.

As part of your learning in Literacy you will look at certain types of non-fiction writing. I'll mention them briefly in the next module, along with purpose, audience and style. The names of the different text types give you clues about their main purposes. When you've got a handle on that, you can understand more easily the

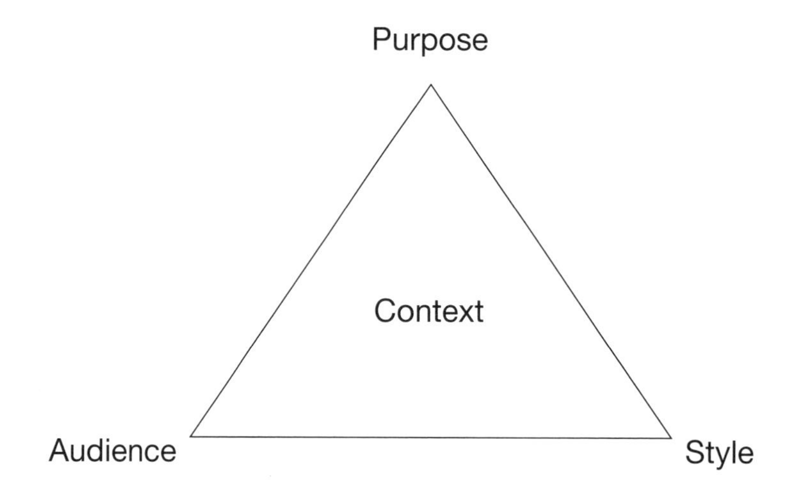

Figure 1

kind of writing style that's most useful. Thinking about your audience will also help you to decide about style.

Use Table 1 as a way of making these decisions.

So just to sum up what we've said . . .

- Decide why you're writing and who you're writing for.
- Base your style on your audience and purpose.

Table 1

Non-fiction text types	**Purpose** – what am I trying to achieve?	**Style** – what would my writing sound like if I read it out loud (i.e. what is the tone of the language)?	**Audience** – who is going to read this (i.e. apart from your teacher, who do you want to influence)?	**Form** – what will my writing look like? (See Table 2 to help you decide.)
Persuading				
Discussing				
Explaining				
Instructing				
Recounting				
Reporting				

- Keep your writing clear and simple. Don't try to show off or confuse.
- Read examples of non-fiction to learn more about how to write it yourself. Ask these questions . . .
  - What is the writer trying to make me think or understand?
  - How is he or she doing this?
  - Where are the facts and opinions? Do these help to make me accept or believe what the writer says?
  - What have I learned from this piece of non-fiction?

Now you can either take a brief look at some different non-fiction text types (**Modules 30–29**), or somersault over to the next block (**Modules 28–24**), which are all about asking questions.

FOR THE PUPIL

Types of non-fiction

Many people interested in your education – including me – are keen that you should become a 'reflective thinker'. Maybe you already are, but if not, when you do, it will mean you'll also be a reflective reader, writer, speaker and listener.

But what does that actually mean? You already know that mirrors reflect light and that you can look at your reflection in them (I do that a lot and think 'Wow, what a handsome guy *he* is!'). But what has the word got to do with thinking? *Reflect* comes from Latin (the language of the Ancient Romans) and literally means 'to bend back'. When we apply it to thinking it means 'to go back and look again' – as you might go back to look at your image in a mirror, where the light is 'bent back' into your eye.

So a reflective thinker is someone who is prepared to go back and look or think again about something – either something you've said or that somebody else has said (verbally or in writing). Being reflective in this way is very important when you come to write non-fiction and when you want to understand non-fiction writing that other people have made. I think it is a *basic skill*. And as you become more skilful at being reflective, you will become a more powerful writer and reader of non-fiction.

But how can I become more reflective, you might ask? (At least I hope you've asked that!). I reckon . . .

- By taking your time to try and work out what the language might mean.
- By noticing, to the best of your ability, how words are being used.
- By asking questions to learn more.
- By realising that facts, opinions, truth, wisdom and lies can be all tangled up together in a piece of non-fiction.
- By reaching decisions based on reasons you've thought about.

Most of this book is about becoming a more reflective thinker. And hey, don't think that you'll wake up one day and be perfect at it. Like most skills, being reflective is like walking along a road that lasts all through your life. Never mind about 'getting there'; just enjoy the journey, I say.

Anyway, what are the different types of non-fiction? In the curriculum you are following they are listed as persuading, instructing, reporting, explaining, recounting and discussing. This isn't necessarily the order in which you'll learn about them, nor are they in order of difficulty. In many cases – in real life anyway – two or more types of non-fiction might be put together. In an advertisement, for instance, you might find elements of both persuasion and explanation. Or in a news report you could find reporting (like, duh!) and recounting. We'll explore the differences between these as we go along.

To finish off this module, here's a little thumbnail sketch of each type:

- **Persuading**. The word (from Latin again) means 'to urge and advise'. Persuasive language usually aims to get you to change your mind about something. Persuasive non-fiction can use logic and reasoning and also try to appeal to your feelings (see **Emotive language** (**Module 19**)).
- **Instructing**. Again, looking at where the word comes from can be helpful. 'Instruct' comes from – you've guessed it, Latin – and means 'to build'. Notice how it's similar to *structure*, something that's built. Instructions, therefore, are like bricks: put them together to build more of an understanding.
- **Reporting**. This word originally meant 'to carry back again'. That makes sense because when you report (news for instance) you carry back ideas, facts, things people have said etc. to an audience that wasn't there at the time. We look at reporting in **Module 3**.
- **Explaining**. An explanation of something is more than just a description of it. So if a description is mainly about *what* something is, an explanation goes further and tells you perhaps *how* it works or *why* it's like that (you might have where, when and who in there as well). One of my favourite pastimes is astronomy. Some nights I go out with a pair of binoculars to look at the stars. If I described my binoculars I'd tell you more about what they looked like. If I *explained* my binoculars I'd also tell you how they work, why they are different from a telescope, and so on.
- **Recounting**. This is also sometimes called *retelling*. Notice the 're' bit, like we saw in reporting. To recount something is to 'tell again' to other people an event or experience. The *count* bit of the word means 'in order', just as when we count numbers we do so in a certain order. So to recount is to retell events in order.
- **Discussing**. This is an 'examination by argument', although it's important to understand that 'argument' doesn't mean having a quarrel, a shouting match or a punch-up. An argument in the true sense means 'to make clear' (from Latin again) through an exchange of ideas, facts and opinions that make up people's different viewpoints. You'll be working on that later – and no arguments!

Types, forms and styles

The different 'text types' can take different forms. By 'form' I mean what the finished piece of writing will look like. So a letter, an article, an essay, a diary extract, a table or chart, a poster, a comic-book layout, a display board, even a poem or a story all count as *forms* that help to make what you want to say more interesting and powerful.

Having said that, if you are asked to write a piece of non-fiction in a test you will possibly be told that it has to take a certain form. An argument will probably take the form of an essay. In creating an advertisement you might be able to put in visuals, such as pictures and different kinds of lettering. Instructions will most likely take the form of a numbered list. These are the *conventional* forms that those types of non-fiction usually take. The word 'convention' means 'coming together in a suitable way'. So conventionally instructions are lists, arguments are written as essays, newspaper reports have a certain structure and layout etc.

All of that is fine and good and helps to make the different non-fiction text types clear in your mind. However, when you do have this clear understanding you can learn even more by being *un*conventional – and it's often fun too. By unconventional I mean deliberately doing things in a different way; putting the text types in unusual forms. Now if you try this you'll find that some ideas work better than others do. I worked in a school once where a class experimented with *recounting* stories from the local newspaper through mime. Another time the pupils created an *argument* about whether homework was a good thing or not (and of course it is!) through an advertising campaign.

There are lots of other combinations you can try. Table 2 might give you some ideas. You can of course add to the list of forms so you have even more choice.

I want to mention one other point here, to do with *style*. Different text types and forms of writing often suit particular styles – or the other way round! A personal letter to a friend, for example, is likely to have a light, friendly, informal style. A letter of complaint to a company – let's say they sent you the wrong item and it was damaged as well – would be the opposite: formal, factual, brief and to the point. You'll realise too that the style is closely linked to the emotional *tone* of the writing. This is like the tone of voice you would use if you read the piece of writing out loud. So the tone of what I'm writing to you now is trying to be friendly, helpful and informal. My writing style is hopefully clear and simple. The text type of this page is a mix of instruction and explanation.

FOR THE PUPIL

Anyway, enough of this for now. Maybe you want to play with the ideas in Table 2 more than anything else in the world! Or perhaps you'd prefer to learn more about asking questions – in which case leap across to the next block of modules.

Table 2

Text Type/ Form	**Persuading**	**Instructing**	**Reporting**	**Explaining**	**Recounting**	**Discussing**
Essay						
List						
Letter						
Article						
News story						
Poster						
Diary						
Chart						
Poster						
Comic						
Drama						
Song						

Section 2 Questioning skills

Be nosy!

Whenever I'm asked to speak to teachers about questioning skills, I recommend three activities that usually (though not always) highlight problems with the current classroom situation.

A question audit

This works best by having a colleague observe a lesson and note down the following information about the 'questioning behaviour' that goes on during a lesson:

- Who asks the questions?
- What kinds of questions are asked, and in what proportion?
- What follows on from the asking of the questions?

When I first did a question audit in my own classroom, many years ago now, it quickly became obvious that *I* asked most of the questions and that these were 'designed' to check whether the pupils had remembered the things I'd told them. The children's questions tended to be procedural and related to the business of the classroom, rather than being self-generated to probe the context of the work we were doing. In other words, their questions would typically be of the 'Can I go to the toilet?/Where's the lined paper?/Darren's flicking my ear, will you tell him to stop sir?' kind.

The follow-on from this rather limited questioning environment was predictable. If a child answered my question with the 'right answer', I'd feel pleased that I'd done my job. If it was the wrong answer, I might think the child had not listened and could well find myself going over the material again. My responses to the procedural questions were geared towards keeping the lesson moving so I could 'cover' the content in the time available.

Frankly these findings shocked me since they so clearly revealed the dominance of my unrelentingly didactic presence in the classroom, the 'coverage of content' model of teaching that was operating and the limited nature of the children's questioning behaviour, which I was doing little to develop.

A cloud of questions

This simple workshop helps to change the situation. The idea is to bring an object into the classroom and encourage the pupils to ask questions about it, as many as possible, with no judgements being made about them (questions or children) and no pressure on anyone to know the answers. I did this with some misgivings the first time because I thought the activity would flop after a couple of minutes as the children ran out of questions to ask. But I was wrong. I put my coffee mug on the desk and said 'Let's see how many questions we can ask about this.' Forty-five minutes and 163 questions later we were still going strong.

What emerged so strikingly from this simple workshop was that the pupils *really enjoyed* asking questions when there was no pressure on them to know the answers already, and when they knew they were not being judged in any way. We all quickly discovered also that questions generate more questions, creating links with many other areas of enquiry and knowledge. Another discovery was that, once we had a mass of questions, we could group them according to difficulty, relevance or 'kind' (open, closed etc.), which in turn led to further discussions about why certain questions were relevant or not, and to whom etc.

A lesson of questions

At first I found this to be quite an unnerving experience, because it challenged my definition of a teacher as necessarily being a repository of knowledge. The idea is to announce to the pupils 'After I have finished saying this, everything else that I say or that any of you say must be in the form of a question.' As soon as the cocky young tyke on the back row says 'Why?' and you say 'What do you think?' the game has begun. Be prepared for long and maybe uncomfortable silences, for frivolous questions, indeed for a certain amount of 'silliness' as pupils too find themselves in this strange situation where they are not routinely being told things but must generate ideas and enquiry for themselves. The only other tip I would offer here is to use your own creativity in framing questions that keep the activity moving.

Once the ethos of what has been called 'the enquiry method' is established, the children's questioning behaviour can be applied to any area of the curriculum, not least developing their skills for understanding and writing non-fiction.

FOR THE PUPIL

Be nosy!

You might have heard of NC – not the National Curriculum, but Natural Curiosity. Human beings (and cats too) have always been curious. It's a habit with us to want to find out more, ranging from what your best friend just wrote about you in their diary, to what lies at the edge of the universe (if the universe has an edge that is . . . I wonder how I can find out?).

I believe very strongly that without our natural curiosity we probably wouldn't have survived as a species. I also think that all of our learning depends upon wanting to find out more and looking for ways of doing that. Two really powerful ways of finding out more are (1) to notice things and (2) to ask questions. These two things are related of course. In fact they're like two sides of the same coin. When you notice things you can use what you've noticed to ask questions. And in trying to answer the questions your attention is often drawn back to what else you can notice.

Activity: Curiosity

Here's an easy game. Take a look at the picture below, Figure 2, and ask as many questions as you can about it. Work with some friends if you want to. And it's also a good idea to record the questions somehow – write them down or record them on a laptop or whatever.

(Tip: don't worry if a question seems silly or trivial. We're really going for sheer quantity in this game!)

OK, well done. Now look at the mass of questions you've made. I'd like you to come to some decisions about them. I want you to decide:

1 Which three questions are the most interesting to you personally?
2 If you were a newspaper reporter, which three questions do you think are the most important ones to ask, and why? (Either decide this by yourself or in discussion with your friends.)
3 How you could possibly begin to find answers to the six questions from answers (1) and (2)?

Now here's one more job to do before moving on to another module . . .

Find any newspaper article that interests you and do the same activity again – think of as many questions to ask about it as you can and answer (1), (2) and (3).

Thanks for that. Your teacher might have a couple more questioning games to try out with you. Or maybe you'll have a chance to go straight to one of the next two modules . . .

Module 28

FOR THE PUPIL

Figure 2

FOR THE TEACHER

Types of question

Categorising questions helps us as teachers to guide and direct pupils towards becoming more effective in their questioning behaviour. Encouraging the children themselves to consider different ways of grouping questions is a useful activity and enables them to understand that questions are like instruments in a box, each having its own particular function. Being able to choose a certain instrument to do a specific job is a vital skill in learning generally, but is especially relevant here as children analyse non-fiction and create and review their own work.

Basic categories of questions include:

- What I call the six big important questions – where, when, what, who, why, how (some people add 'which'). An elaboration of the idea is known as the Questions Matrix. This is a grid of thirty-six question starters that cross-reference present/past/possibility/probability/prediction/imagination (vertical axis) with event/situation/choice/person/reason/means (horizontal axis). Cross-matching present with event therefore forms the question 'What is (happening)?', while cross-matching imagination with person generates 'Who might (turn up at the party)?' An internet search will locate the matrix in seconds; for example go to www.sci.tamucc.edu/~eyoung/4382/question_matrix.html.
- Closed and open questions. Closed questions are those that require a short (and preferably right) answer or a yes/no response. Their principal value lies in coming straight to the point. Thus they are useful in eliciting precise pieces of information and moving on swiftly in a discussion. The reply to one closed question can often trigger another one and then another, such that chain of linked questions is generated. Examining such a question-chain reveals the sometimes very sophisticated thinking of the questioner. Play the *Twenty (Closed) Questions* game (described in the pupil notes) with the class to introduce or reinforce closed questioning. Another useful activity is to watch video clips of court cases – these are likely to be fictional and dramatised, but clearly show how such questions can 'probe and cut' like surgical instruments to uncover the facts of the case.
- Open questions, as the name indicates, can accommodate many answers, which may be facts, opinions or a mixture of these. They may be 'small-chunk' or 'big-chunk' questions, depending on the scale or breadth of response the questioner wishes to elicit. A small-chunk question might be 'What do you

think we could have for tea this evening?' A big-chunk question could be 'What might be done to offset the effects of global warming?'

- Lower- and higher-order questions. These categories refer to Benjamin Bloom's taxonomy of thinking (see Bibliography), which is a model that identifies different kinds of thinking along a continuum from simple thinking/little understanding towards complex thinking/greater understanding.
  - Lower-order questions seek knowledge, comprehension and application, so here we would find questions such as 'How many times does the writer use the word "because" in his article?'/'Why does using "because" make an argument stronger?'/'What other ways of making an argument stronger can you think of?'
  - Higher-order questions seek analysis, synthesis and evaluation, thus – 'How can we go about deciding what is fact and what is opinion in the article we've just read?'/'What theme would be a useful one to pick when writing an article of our own, and how would we go about preparing it?'/'Do you agree with the writer's argument in the article, and what are the reasons behind your answer?'

  To learn more about Bloom's model either seek out his *Taxonomy of Educational Objectives* or, for a more succinct account, Mel Rockett and Simon Percival's *Thinking for Learning* (see Bibliography).
- Rhetorical questions are aimed at the emotions and don't usually require an answer. I've heard that some teachers use them as a tool for behaviour management ('Tyler, do you intend to sit around doing nothing *all* lesson?'). Children need to know about them as they are used as a persuasive device in arguments (and so that Tyler doesn't make the mistake of answering 'yes').
- Meta-model questions. This idea arises out of work done in the field of Neuro-Linguistic Programming by Richard Bandler and John Grinder, which itself stemmed from Noam Chomsky's earlier work on transformational grammar. Bandler and Grinder recognised that when we talk or write about our experience we tend to distort, delete and generalise the information. The Meta model uses questioning to fill in missing details by clarifying ambiguities, identifying presuppositions, dissolving conflicts and highlighting inconsistencies. Meta-model questions tend to feature terms such as exactly, precisely, explain in more detail, tell me more about, what are the reasons for etc. A simple example is given in the pupil notes on page 36.

Incidentally, a very useful book on questioning is Norah Morgan and Juliana Saxton's *Asking Better Questions* (see Bibliography). For more on Meta-model questioning see the teacher's notes for **Oh yes it is! Oh no it isn't!** (**Module 15**).

FOR THE PUPIL

Types of question

A friend of mine, a lady called Sara Stanley, invented a character called Philosophy Bear. He is best mates with a character I invented, a cat called Pinkerton. While Pinkerton likes being nosy by noticing things, Philosophy Bear is nosy – or maybe inquisitive is a better word – by asking questions. As time went by he discovered several useful things about questions . . .

- Some questions have one right answer – for example, what is the capital of England? (A kid in a class I visited said 'E' and got into trouble with her teacher for it.)
- Some questions have lots of right answers – ask ten of your friends what is their favourite food and you might get ten different answers.
- Some questions have no absolutely 'right' answers but different answers depending upon your viewpoint – so what is the position of the sun in the sky right now? Answer: it depends where you're standing. Another example: Do you think that there are too many tests in school? Answer: it depends on who you ask, what you mean by 'too many', even what you mean by 'tests' etc.
- The answer you get sometimes depends on the way you ask the question. There is a kind of question called a *polar question*, which tries to persuade you to answer yes or no, or true or false. You often find these in questionnaires and surveys. So, for example, are sweets bad for you? Now my reaction (and maybe yours) is 'Well, it depends.' But in surveys you are usually asked to tick a yes/no box to give your answer, with no room to write what you think in any detail.
- Some questions are *unanswerable*. This is to say that, although people have been talking about them for hundreds and even thousands of years, we are no closer to knowing the answer for sure. Such questions are often called 'philosophical questions' (which is how Philosophy Bear got his name). They are more to do with talking about what people mean by certain words and exploring possible answers. Very often questions like this throw up lots more questions and often lead people to say 'Well, it depends . . .'. Here are some examples of philosophical questions.
  - How do I know I am me?
  - Where does the universe end?
  - Is the act of killing a person *always* wrong?
  - Does God exist?

- How do I know that the world (and that includes you and me) isn't a dream?
- What is the difference between a live rat and a dead rat?

You might like to pick one of these and talk about it with your friends for a little while. How many other questions come out of your discussion?

(Tip for the teacher: if you want to explore philosophical enquiry further with your class, I recommend Sara Stanley's and my *But Why?* teaching pack, which includes four picture books, one of which features Philosophy Bear. Also useful are Stephen Law's *Philosophy Files 1 & 2* (see Bibliography).)

There are two other kinds of questions I want to mention just here. One could be called the *probing question* (your teacher might call it a Meta-model question). This is where somebody says something rather vague and your job is to get more exact information from him or her.

So, for example, if a person says 'You can't trust people from the North!', what questions could you ask to get a clearer idea of what they mean? (Tip: use words like 'exactly' and 'precisely' and phrases like 'explain in more detail' or 'give some examples'.)

Activity: Questions

Finally we'll visit yes/no questions. These are also called *closed questions*. Here's a game to play. Look at the grid on page 37 (Figure 3). The game is called *Twenty (Closed) Questions*. Pick one of the pictures or words. Your friends have to work out which one you've chosen by asking *clear and precise questions* that can be answered yes or no – no guessing allowed.

When you've played the game, talk about which questions were the most useful and why.

After the activity, move on to the next module . . .

Figure 3

Modules 26–25

FOR THE TEACHER

Some principles of discovery learning

Many educationalists recognise that children's ability to learn is enhanced when they feel comfortable in an environment of ambiguity and uncertainty – in other words when they are not under pressure to 'know the right answer right now'. One great drawback of the current content-driven curriculum is that it is packed with knowledge that has to be 'covered' by the teacher and subsequently remembered by the students in order for them to be judged to have reached a certain level of competence or mastery of the subject. The questioning of the veracity or relevance of such knowledge is rarely given the same emphasis.

While there is nothing wrong with knowledge per se, I think there is a great deal to be concerned about when classroom environments value children's ability to reiterate facts above their willingness to question information presented to them. And I don't just mean questioning particular snippets of information, but at the very least having an awareness of the notion that the whole curriculum represents *someone else's opinion of what is worth knowing*. This is a huge and controversial subject and its exploration falls outside the scope of this book. If you are interested in delving deeper, however, I recommend the work of John Abbot and *Teaching as a Subversive Activity* by Postman and Weingartner (especially the chapter called 'What's worth knowing?'), both previously mentioned.

While it may not be helpful to encourage children to question the very bases on which their schooling is built (though some would disagree), for the age range we are concerned with I think it is not only useful but also necessary for pupils to be aware that:

- Many 'right answers' have come about after a long process of questioning, doubting and challenging previously believed 'truths'.
- 'The truth' is often partial, provisional and relative, based on our current level of understanding.
- Knowledge can have spin (like cricket balls) and be a subtle blend of factual information and opinion that is sometimes based on vested interests. Facts themselves may be the products of interpretation, distortion, deletion and generalisation – in other words, the outcomes of the way the human brain filters 'reality'.

FOR THE TEACHER

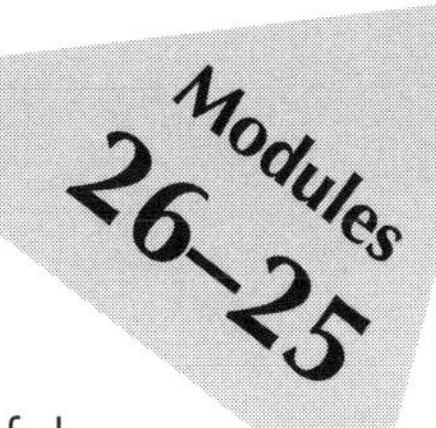

- Open-minded scepticism (which presupposes inquisitiveness) is a more useful and powerful attitude when dealing with information than gullibility and the passive acceptance of facts.
- It's OK not to know the right answer, or all of the answers, right now. This is most immediately important to our purposes of enabling children to engage with factual information, in both its construction and analysis.
- All of the above constitute a 'knowingness' (based implicitly on Sturgeon's first two laws) that information, like plasticine, can be shaped and moulded to suit different purposes and agendas.
- Inquisitiveness, directed through reflective questioning, is a self-sharpening instrument. Over time questions become more incisive and powerful.

It's OK not to know

1 How many people are there in the world today?
2 Is space travel a good thing?
3 Do you think that space travel is a good thing?
4 What does it mean to be educated?
5 What are the first ten prime numbers?

Finally,

6 If you don't know the answers to the first five questions, how do you feel about that?

This module is called 'It's OK not to know'. But I have to say a few other things about that to make myself clear. Often in school you are expected to be able to remember facts that your teachers have told you. If you remember those facts well and can write them out in a test, you gain a high mark and everyone is pleased. Because your teachers and other adults – and you too I hope – *want* you to do well at school, knowing such facts and being able to come up with the right answers to test questions becomes important. In that sense, it's not OK (in all sorts of ways) if you 'don't know'.

But as part of your learning, and in your life more generally, not knowing a right answer is not always a bad thing. However, feeling comfortable not to know the answer right now is part of a bigger and very important attitude that lies at the heart of this book. It's OK not to know if:

- You are willing to find out more in searching for the truth (or at least greater understanding).
- You understand that the 'right answer' for one person might not be the right answer for someone else.
- You realise that asking questions is a powerful way to learn more.
- You are prepared to play with ideas, facts, opinions and information to see how they can fit together in different ways.

So – if you felt bad about not knowing the answers to questions 1–5 above, there's no need. And if you felt OK about not knowing the answers, that's fine, as long as you are prepared to seek out the answers.

One useful way of doing that is to look closely at each question to see what it's 'up to'. Let's take a quick look at them again – check out Table 3.

Table 3

The question	My thoughts about it	How can we find out more?
1 How many people are there in the world today?	The question sounds as though it ought to have a definite answer. But does every country keep a count of all the people who live there? Also, the answer to this question will keep changing all the time as the world's population increases. Perhaps any answer can only be an estimate.	Maybe look at various estimates and take an average. ▶ Where would we find such estimates? ▶ How do we know they are 'true'? ▶ Do we need to give an exact answer to this question?
2 Is space travel a good thing?	This question seems simple and straightforward. But 'good' is such a vague word. Good for whom? And in what ways? Could any answer, even if it was supported by facts, be anything more than an opinion?	Maybe ask different people for their opinions and present their answers as a kind of discussion or list, 'for' and 'against'.
3 Do you think that space travel is a good thing?	Notice how this question is different from the last one. This time you are being asked to give *your own personal opinion*.	I think that intelligent people would respect your opinion even if they disagreed with it. Find out what you think and how you feel by maybe doing a mind map that breaks this big topic down into smaller bits (see the next module). Whatever your opinion is, it will carry more weight if you give reasons for what you think.
4 What does it mean to be educated?	This is another vague question, since 'educated' can mean so many different things.	▶ Maybe look up the word educated in a dictionary. ▶ Maybe ask for different people's opinions. ▶ Maybe state what you already think, giving your reasons. ▶ Maybe – if it's possible – ask the questioner to be more precise.
5 What are the first ten prime numbers?	Well, I don't know the answer! But I do know that it's a question that has a definite right answer.	Simply look up the answer in a Maths book. But I would look in a couple of other places to check that the answer is correct.

What we can usefully learn from this is that even questions that seem to be short, simple and straightforward might have 'hidden depths' and be more complicated than we first thought. The way to tackle such questions is to unwrap them and find out what answering them might involve.

If you want to have a go at this jump to the next module – **Yes, but what does it mean?** This will lead you on to the module after that, which is also about questions.

Or you might prefer to leap to the next block (**Modules 23–19**), which looks in some detail at how words can play tricks with us.

Yes, but what does it mean?

Is space travel a good thing?

How easy it is to answer 'yes' or 'no' or 'it depends' and then get on with your life! And how sad it is (in my opinion) to answer 'I don't know' or – even sadder – 'I don't care'. Don't get me wrong. What I mean is that I think it's sad if a person doesn't know *and isn't interested in finding out more*. And I think not caring is sadder if it's part of a general attitude of *not being bothered about much at all*. I believe that people who don't want to know and aren't bothered anyway are pretty vulnerable: I think they are easily led because they are not thinking for themselves. Maybe you disagree. If you do, that's fine because at least you've bothered about it!

Activity: What does the question mean?

Anyway, back to whether space travel is a good thing. Before we can form a reasoned answer it makes sense to explore what the question could mean. A first step is to make some observations and ask some further questions about it. If you can think of any jot them down now before looking at my first thoughts.

- **Observation**. The question sounds as though it's looking for a yes/no answer. But I think the topic is more complicated than that. Straightaway I'm thinking 'it depends'.
- **Question**. Does the question mean space travel generally? Because there are different kinds of space travel. There's manned and unmanned (i.e. robot craft). There are military spacecraft (such as spy satellites) and scientific spacecraft (such as the Hubble Space Telescope). And there are satellites that do a job that's obviously useful – such as looking out for hurricanes on Earth, and space probes that gather information that has no obvious practical value yet – such as photographing distant galaxies.
- **Observation and questions**. The word 'good' is very vague – it's what I call a *slippery* word (see **Module 20**). We need to question that word further. So:
  - Good in what way(s)?
  - Good for whom?
  - What other words would be clearer than 'good'?

Now maybe the person asking the question isn't present, in which case *we* would have to provide answers to our own questions. We can also ask about the *context* of the question (remember that word 'context'?). So:

- Who is asking the question?
- Why is the question being asked?
- How will our answers be used?

These kinds of questions become especially important when we begin to think about how advertisements, questionnaires and other people with vested interests try to influence us – ask your teacher what 'vested interests' means. But it's good practice to ask these kinds of questions anyway.

By taking this approach we succeed in breaking down a big, vague idea into a number of smaller and clearer ones. Now we are in a better position to frame an answer.

If you are being asked for your personal opinion, you must still give reasons for the way you think and feel. If you are being asked to answer more generally, you must present a *balanced argument* that explores both sides of the issue ('Yes, space travel is a good thing because . . .' *versus* 'No, it's a bad thing because . . .'). If you want to have a go at this now have a look at the 'Car Parking Charges' material on the website.

(Tip for the teacher: the website link also features a couple of other reasoning and discussion activities – a debate about meat eating and a mystery to solve: 'Who Stole the Kay-to-Bah Diamond?')

A useful next step is to keep the *if-then-I think-because* formula in mind. This focuses your mind on the details, allows you to have an opinion and includes a reason. So:

- If you mean manned space exploration then I think it is a good thing because a human being can find out more than robot explorers. Or . . .
- I think manned exploration is a bad thing because it is much more expensive than using robot explorers and the money could be spent more usefully on other things.

Before going any further, I wonder if you can use find any questions to ask about the two points above?

Now you can practise the *if-then-I think-because* technique further on this question. Or you might prefer to visit **Module 24**, which takes the idea further. Or you can zoom to the next block of modules beginning with **Module 23**, which looks at how you can check out information.

FOR THE TEACHER

Going after the meaning

In his wonderfully angry yet funny book *Gobbledygook* (see Bibliography), Don Watson makes the important point that, if we use words to seek truth, preserving the clarity and straightforwardness of language is vital: by holding the simple belief that truth is worth preserving we are compelled to respect language. George Orwell argued a similar point over half a century earlier, when he asserted that the slovenliness of our language makes it easier for us to have foolish thoughts (see the essay 'Politics and the English language' – http://orwell.ru/library/essays/politics/english/e_polit).

I think we need to consider two aspects of this idea as we help children to become more powerful readers and writers of 'non-fiction'. First, there is the notion of valuing 'transparent' language per se – language that tries to be clear and straightforward based on the desire for precise and accurate communication. Then there is the issue of engaging with language that is deliberately vague, overblown, impersonal or emotive for a variety of reasons, which often have to do with influencing people in ways that are not open, honest and transparent. When encouraging children to write non-fiction, the rule of thumb 'keep it plain and simple' will stand them in good stead. And in reading non-fiction we can advise children to 'make it plain and simple' by going after the meaning through questioning, doubting, challenging – the strategy forming the backbone of this book.

There are several features of language use that we can focus on in developing our children's critical eye:

- Errors (often but not always unintentional) of spelling, punctuation and sentence construction.
- Vagueness and ambiguity.
- Use of jargon and a high-flown, impersonal style (typically found in the language of bureaucracy, including education alas – the 'management speak' so reviled by Don Watson).
- Emotive language.

These and other characteristics of unclear language can occur in combination of course, making the message even more elegantly devious or self-important or perhaps just blunderingly complicated and confusing. While all of this constitutes a serious issue in terms of children's language education, my feeling is that cultivating an attitude of playful curiosity in them is the most effective and enjoyable way of tackling the matter.

Further references: John Humphrys' *Lost for Words* is a brilliantly grumpy and hugely informative survey of slovenliness in our language. Also recommended are Bill Bryson's *Mother Tongue* and William Strunk and E.B. White's *The Elements of Style*, which is a brief but invaluable sourcebook for writing simply and clearly (see Bibliography).

Going after the meaning

I visited a school recently and one of the kids had pinned this notice to the door of the staffroom:

Warning! May contain nuts.

Can you see why that is funny? If you can't, ask your teacher to explain. The message contains two meanings, which hinge on the word 'nuts'. Nuts can be a kind of food, like peanuts, brazil nuts, walnuts etc.; and the word can also mean people who are 'nutty' or crazy. Of course the idea's not so funny if you have to explain it. But the point I want to make is that it's possible to look at or *interpret* the sentence in those two ways.

Interpreting is trying to work out what something means; to 'translate' a message so that it's clear in your mind. When you create your own non-fiction, your teacher and I will encourage you to write in a way that's already clear and simple, so that your readers will have little difficulty in interpreting what you say. When you read non-fiction, our advice – and you've come across it before – is to **be nosy!** Notice things and ask questions.

Activity: Interpretation

Let's practise that a bit now. Can you notice anything odd or funny in these phrases and sentences? The first three are newspaper headlines:

1 Tonight – Special Concert by the London Sympathy Orchestra.
2 Police Appeal for Witnesses – Four People Battered in Fish Shop.
3 Local Nurse Helps Dog Bite Victim.
4 Slow children at play.
5 'I once shot an elephant in my pyjamas.'
6 Children hate annoying teachers.
7 Dogs must be carried on the escalator.

All of these are funny, although a few didn't intend to be. Here's why . . .

1 'Sympathy' is the wrong word to use. It should be 'symphony' (ask your teacher to tell you about something called malapropisms).

2 'Battered' can mean 'beaten up', which was what the headline meant to say. Or it can mean 'covered in batter'. The fact that the incident happened in a fish shop makes the joke.

3 This sounds as though the nurse helped a dog to bite a victim. The intended meaning would be clear by using a hyphen: Local Nurse Helps Dog-Bite Victim (i.e. the victim who was bitten by a dog).

4 The sentence suggests that the children are slow. An exclamation mark would make the intended meaning clear – Slow! Children at play.

5 A famous comedian called Groucho Marx said this and then added, 'I have no idea what the elephant was doing in my pyjamas.' Try rewriting the sentence the make its intended meaning clearer.

6 When a sentence can have two (or more) meanings it is said to be *ambiguous*. This example is ambiguous because it could mean:

- Children hate annoying their teachers.
- Children hate teachers who are annoying.

7 This sentence is ambiguous too. Can you work out why?

The sentences we've looked at play tricks on you, either on purpose or accidentally. I hope you chuckled at them anyway. But sometimes the tricks in non-fiction are there deliberately to influence you in one way or another. Now that's a serious matter – and we'll be investigating it in the next block of modules. Ask your teacher to help you decide which module to look at now.

Section 3 Evaluating information

How do we know?

I once visited a school as part of their Science Week: as a 'real live' author I was there to talk about how scientific ideas can be used in science fiction stories. I happened to be sitting in on a Y5 Astronomy lesson, during the course of which the class teacher stated that 'light travels in straight lines'. Immediately one girl asked 'How do we know?' The teacher was honest enough (or astute enough) to admit that she'd read it in her syllabus notes. With very little prompting the same pupil, with a wry grin, asked 'How do we know *they* are right?'

It was a pertinent question. The rest of the lesson was spent talking about how we might check the accuracy of the idea that light travels in straight lines, which led to further discussion on how we could discover the veracity of *any* information presented to us. It seemed to me that, by then, the children were 'doing science' in a far more relevant and useful way than simply being told scientific facts.

We are of course surrounded by information – millions of facts that these days become available at the click of a mouse. I have suggested earlier in the pupil notes that language can 'play tricks on you', although sometimes information does not deliberately intend to deceive: it is just out of date, incomplete, simplistic, unintentionally biased or simply irrelevant to the user's purpose. When children think to ask 'How do we know?' they are displaying a healthy change in attitude away from being passive recipients of ideas to being active seekers of truth.

A useful first step in helping children to evaluate information is to introduce them to the CARR model – Currency, Accuracy/Reliability, Relevance:

- **Currency** (or recency). How up to date is the information? How much does that matter? In some subjects or topics information is changing very rapidly as new discoveries are made, while in other areas facts and ideas can remain 'stable' for much longer.

- **Accuracy/reliability**. How do we know that the information is 'right' or 'true'? What are the author's qualifications and professional background? What sources (if any) are quoted? Where else can the information be checked? (Note that accuracy and reliability are sometimes considered together under the heading of 'Authority'.)
- **Relevance**. How useful/appropriate is this information for my needs? Is the source of information (book, article, website etc.) too general or detailed? Is the information pitched at the right level (i.e. can I understand it!)? What is the intended audience of the information? Do the questions I asked about currency and accuracy/reliability help me to decide if the information is relevant?

Note: By the way, if you are interested is using SF to teach science, an interesting workbook is Julie Czerneda's *No Limits: Developing scientific literacy using science fiction* (see Bibliography).

How do we know?

OK, before we go any further, look back at the title of this block of modules, **Evaluating information** – what does that title mean? If you've got the attitude we're recommending in this book (noticing, questioning, challenging) you'll have asked that question already. There's no benefit in skipping words you don't understand, and no point in using them in your work either.

Evaluating means assessing the value of something. Information is knowledge that has some practical value or that leads to greater understanding. In order to write non-fiction, often you have to use facts and ideas that you've found elsewhere – in books, on the Internet and so on. If you don't check (or evaluate) those facts, your explanation, discussion or instructions could be weakened if they are inaccurate or just plain wrong.

So in this case the value of the information you check is related to how well it supports your writing. But how can you assess ideas to see if they are accurate or right or true? Have a chat with your friends and jot your thoughts down. Compare what you think with other groups and make a list.

You might well find that what you have decided fits well with what I'm calling the CARR plan. Those letters stand for:

- How **C**urrent or 'up to date' is the information?
- How **A**ccurate or 'correct' are the facts?
- How **R**eliable or 'trustworthy' are the places where you found the facts?
- How **R**elevant or 'to the point' are the facts to the points you want to make?

These four 'benchmarks' work together. You might think that the encyclopaedias in your library (sorry, learning resource centre) are a reliable source of information. But if the books are old the facts you find might not be current. If, for example, you were writing about the problem of famine across the globe and wanted to mention the world's population, you'd find that the figure in a book that's more than a few years old would be wrong. Some areas of knowledge change quickly so the rule here is:

If in doubt, check it out.

So just to sum up, here are a few big Dos (I stepped in something similar last week):

- Do check your facts, and in more than one place.
- Do check them according to CARR.
- Do put information into your own words (if you can) when you use it in your work.

And a few big Don'ts:

- Don't skip or use words you haven't understood.
- Don't copy and paste great slabs of writing from the Internet into your work.
- Don't hesitate to share your sweets with your teacher.

Activity: Check it out

Anyway, that's enough laying down the law. Have a look at this sentence:

Elephants Please Stay In Your Car!

It was a sign painted in a safari park. As it stands, what does it mean? What do you think the signwriter intended it to mean? I hope you agree with me that it should be:

Elephants. Please Stay In Your Car!

What a difference a dot makes. We'll take a closer look at this idea in the next module . . .

FOR THE PUPIL

Slippery meanings

(There are no teacher's notes for this module.)

I was sitting in a café at a railway station recently and I noticed this sign:

Meal Deal! Only £2.99 for a breakfast roll and med hot coffee!

What do you think it means? Put it in your own words. Could the sign be taken to mean anything different? How do you think the way the sign is written is trying to persuade you to buy the meal deal? Have a chat with your classmates about this and then you might want to glance at the thoughts I had . . .

- Notice the use of capital letters on Meal Deal. Capitals are often used to suggest importance or something special, which is why we use them for proper nouns – the names of particular people, places and things.
- Notice the use of exclamation marks (!). These usually show emotions: the word exclaim comes from the Latin 'to cry out'. In this case the two exclamation marks are, I think, trying to create a sense of excitement and 'Wow, what a bargain'.
- Notice the word 'only', which is trying to suggest that £2.99 is a very good price to pay for your roll and coffee.
- Notice how £2.99 sounds and looks quite a lot less than £3.00. This is a common trick in advertising, where items are priced just short of the nearest pound or dollar. The idea behind it is that we notice (in this case) the £2 and don't think that we're only a penny away from £3.
- Notice the use of the adjective 'hot'. Of course the word lets you know that you're not getting iced coffee, but it's also there to tempt you. 'Hot coffee' sounds cosier and more delicious than just plain 'coffee' (especially since it was a cold morning outside when I read the sign.)

We'll be exploring these ideas in more detail later. But for now I want you to concentrate on that phrase 'med hot coffee'. The chances are it means 'a medium-sized cup of hot coffee'. But it could be taken to mean:

- 'a cup of medium-quality hot coffee'. That meaning would be clearer if the sentence was written as 'a cup of medium, hot coffee.'

- 'a mediocre (average) cup of hot coffee'. That meaning would be clearer if 'med' were written as 'mediocre'.

The fact that you probably opted for the intended meaning means that you made decisions about the words, maybe without even realising it. We read notices and signs all the time and 'get what they mean' usually without any problems. However, there are a few important ideas lying behind what we've looked at in this module:

- For various reasons, information that we come across is often *distorted* or 'twisted out of shape'. Mainly this takes the form of some information being left out (this is called 'deletion') and information being vague (this is called 'generalisation' – general or broad ideas being based on little bits of information). Again we'll look at this idea later.
- We have to make decisions all the time about what language means. The more deliberately and flexibly we do this, in my opinion, the less chance there is that we'll be tricked by language. By looking 'flexibly' at language I mean trying to explore the different meanings that words, phrases and sentences could take.
- Sometimes language doesn't try to trick us; it simply hasn't been written clearly enough. But all too often language is *deliberately designed* to influence us in some way, as in the breakfast roll sign above. When we read non-fiction, we should be aware of this. When we write non-fiction, we can deliberately use any of the tricks to make what we say more persuasive.

When language can take more than one meaning (on purpose or accidentally) it is said to be *ambiguous*. The word (from the Latin) means 'to lead', which I think is interesting. Perhaps it suggests that deliberately ambiguous language is trying to lead our minds in a certain direction?

Activity: Ambiguity

Anyway, here are a few ambiguous sentences, some of which you may have met earlier. See if you can work out a couple of possible meanings for each:

- Zoo Keeper Attacked By Elephant in Pyjamas!
- Dogs must be carried on the escalator.

FOR THE PUPIL

- After use, staff should empty the teapot and stand upside down on the draining board.
- If you are offended by our waiters, you should see the manager.

If you want to learn more about how to deal with ambiguous language, take the escalator to the next module, **21** (be sure to carry a dog!). If you want to find out about how language can affect your feelings, take a look at **Module 19**.

FOR THE TEACHER

How to be a Doubting Thomas

Developing children's interpretative abilities is a key feature in enabling pupils to both 'decode' non-fiction and write their own. Once they begin to ask for themselves 'What is this language trying to say/make me think, feel or do?', that major insight opens the door to purposeful exploration of the way non-fiction blends text type, form, style and intention. In that sense all language is influential and, as I've suggested in the pupil pages, sometimes it deliberately tries to 'play tricks', and for less than noble purposes. I feel very strongly that children should have a 'working awareness' of this, one that leads to a useful balance between open-mindedness and hard-nosed scepticism. As someone once said, you don't want to be so open-minded that your wits fall out. On the other hand, an entrenched stance similarly limits a person's ability to make reasoned decisions about the ideas they encounter. In another but not unrelated context, in Postman and Weingartner's aforementioned book (see Bibliography) they describe this attitude as a 'hardening of the categories', where in more extreme cases the individual refuses to consider any new ideas that are not congruent with their previously established (and unmovable) beliefs. Such an unreasonable and unreasoning stance can be seen in all areas of human discussion. The history of scientific discovery, for instance, is riddled with stories of highly intelligent, learned men and women refusing to consider new facts, reacting instead with blind rage to any challenge to what they feel to be 'the truth'. This has led several commentators to note that science progresses only because of the death of old scientists. An excessive statement . . . perhaps.

Implicit in the above is the assertion that, as children become more 'savvy' in handling non-fiction presented to them in English/literacy lessons, the thinking skills they are developing will be just as useful in many other areas of the curriculum. There is currently, for example, intense controversy in some parts of America about whether Creationism should be taught alongside evolutionary theory as an explanation of 'how we came to be here'. I wonder how you feel about this? And I wonder if your viewpoint would shift if most or all children were able to reach reasoned conclusions in this and other matters for themselves?

A useful tool, I've found, is the Four Roles/Resources of the Reader model developed in the early 1990s by Peter Freebody and Allan Luke (see Bibliography), which works equally well for both non-fiction and fictional text. The four roles/resources are:

- **Code breaker** (decoder) – decoding the codes and conventions of written forms.
- **Text user** (illustrator) – understanding the various cultural/social functions of different texts.
- **Text participant** (discussion manager) – actively and incisively comprehending texts.
- **Text analyst** (investigator) – understanding and assessing how texts attempt to 'position' or influence readers and listeners.

For more details go to www. decs.sa.gov.au/thenetwork/files/pages/identity_web/LiteracyAsASocialPractice/Fouroles.pdf.

FOR THE PUPIL

How to be a Doubting Thomas

We've already looked at big, basic differences between ideas – whether the things you read or hear are true or false, or facts or fictions, or a mixture of these. We've also explored how language can play tricks on you, sometimes on purpose and sometimes unwittingly. Perhaps to be fairer I should say that language often tries to *influence* us, to make us have certain thoughts and feelings and to make us want to do certain things.

In the same way, often when we speak or write we are trying to do that too. If I read and enjoy a book I will recommend it to other people. And although I can give reasons why I thought the book was good, behind those reasons (which may be 'facts') there is my desire to persuade people to read the book too. I am trying to influence their thoughts, feelings and actions.

In my opinion, in this case it's not a bad thing. But what if I held strong political or religious views and tried in all sorts of ways to use language to get you to believe the same things? Would that be a good or a bad thing, do you think? Or maybe it's more complicated than simply 'good' or 'bad'? Would you feel differently about what I was up to if you already held the same views?

When we come across language that tries to influence us it's possible to react in various ways. We can think:

- OK, I'll believe all of that.
- Huh, I don't believe any of that stuff!
- I'll consider what you've said and make up my own mind, for reasons I've thought about.

Since you've got to know me a bit by now, you've probably guessed that I think the last option is the best one. By 'best' I mean it makes you more powerful and independent, because you've used your intelligence to decide for yourself.

When people are easily led they are said to be *gullible*. The dictionary (www.dictionary.com) says that 'gullible' means easily deceived and cheated. The 'gull' part means to swallow or guzzle, so possibly the idea of gullible is that some folks swallow ideas whole without 'chewing them over'.

FOR THE PUPIL

Module 21

The opposite of gullible is *sceptical*. However, some people are sceptical to the point where they won't even consider ideas that don't fit with what they already believe. That's like building a wall around yourself so that nothing new can get into your mind. But there is such a thing as *open-minded scepticism*. This is an attitude – a useful one, I think – where you don't automatically believe or disbelieve ideas you hear or read, but think about them first. In fact, the true meaning of the word 'sceptic' is 'thoughtful' and before that (from the Greek) 'to look and consider'.

In the next couple of modules we'll take a closer look at how you can be sceptical in that way. By the way, the phrase 'Doubting Thomas' comes from Thomas the Apostle who doubted that Jesus had been resurrected (come back from the dead).

Reading between the lines – slippery words and emotive language

As the author Roy van den Brink-Budgen points out in *Critical Thinking for Students* (see Bibliography), language rarely takes a 'pure' form: a reasoned argument may be laced with emotive language, persuader words, analogies and so-called 'familiar appeals' to authority or tradition etc. (more on this later). Similarly, language that intentionally aims to exert an influence through the emotions may be supported by carefully argued interlinked points, logically drawn conclusions and a raft of thoroughly researched facts. In other words, the 'language of influence' can be a subtle and complex blend of the subjective and the objective, appealing to both the head and the heart at the same time.

Children often find the concept itself difficult to grasp, even before they develop the capabilities of discriminating between the head/heart influences of words they hear or see. As we touched upon in earlier modules, the distinction between fact and opinion, fiction and non-fiction may be blurred and, indeed, these can be used elegantly together to great effect. This is something many children fail to appreciate. An even more basic idea about 'what is true' can also be a stumbling block until children begin to realise that 'facts' are an attempt to reach for truth and are often an approximation based on our current understanding; and also that material can be metaphorically or figuratively true . . .

When I visit schools, I sometimes tell a story about a new boy who found it impossible to fit in, and was teased and bullied.* He had a special gift of being able to mould his flesh into any shape. But whoever he tried to be and however much he tried to 'fit the mould' he was still rejected by the other kids.

Invariably somebody in the audience will ask 'Was that true?' and I've even had that question from adults. All of the modules in this book aim to contribute to the central endeavour of allowing children to understand that *truth is fuzzy*, often based on interpretation, and that feelings as well as facts are used to help shape our values, attitudes and beliefs based on what we feel to be true.

(* The story is called *Gurney* from my *Catch & Other Stories* – see Bibliography.)

Reading between the lines – and slippery words

Have you ever thought about that phrase, 'reading between the lines'? What do you think it means? As you read this page there's nothing actually between the lines except white space: the phrase is not *literally* (or actually) true, but true in another kind of way. I think 'reading between the lines' means that there are ideas and influences hidden within the language. Think back to that notice for a meal deal in **Module 22** – *Only £2.99 for a breakfast roll and med hot coffee!* The way the notice is written tries to tempt you to buy the breakfast roll.

But you might argue (and I hope you do) that there's nothing 'hidden' in the message. All the words are clear on the page. In fact you might think it's a good deal. But compare what's written with this – 'Buy a roll and coffee for £3'. Are you just as tempted? Or what if we went the other way and really turned up the temptation factor – 'Enjoy a fresh, soft, deep-fill breakfast roll and a cup of steaming hot coffee (made with the finest roasted coffee beans) – all for only £2.99!!' Yummy, I've made myself dribble.

Activity: *Read between the lines*

It's usually pretty easy to read between the lines of advertisements and spot how they are trying to get you to buy. We'll look in more detail at that later. For now, read between the lines of these examples. How is language being used to tempt you?

- Check out our exclusive offers. Prices from only £2.99!
- A massive 10% off selected items! But hurry while stocks last.
- Buy one get one free.
- Of course, we don't want to leave our loyal customers out in the cold – so give us a call to chat about what's available exclusively for you.

You'll find loads of other examples by browsing adverts in newspapers and magazines – but hurry while stocks last!!

Activity

Learning to read between the lines is useful not just when investigating commercials. There are 'hidden influences' in many forms of language. One common example is the use of what I call 'slippery' words. These sound positive, powerful and persuasive but tend to be vague (partly because they can mean so many different things). The word *good* comes under this heading. Talk about what the word good can mean in the following phrases:

- A good idea.
- A good meal.
- Good behaviour.
- A good argument.
- Good heavens!
- Good-for-nothing.

The word *best* is slippery too. Think of a few phrases where the word appears and chat with your friends about its different shades of meaning.

Now check out **Module 19**, where we begin to look at how language sometimes tries to influence your feelings.

Emotive language

Did you take time to notice that word 'emotive'? What do you think it means? It sounds similar to words like emotions, motives, motivation, motion and even motor. A big clue is in that last word, because a motor is designed to move things. In fact all of these words are to do with moving.

Have you heard the expression being 'moved to tears'? Or 'it was a very moving experience'? In what way is that word 'moving' being used, do you think? If someone is 'moved to act' then what they experience causes them to do something. And, at the heart of it, what moves us are our feelings – or emotions – which form our natural reactions to the things that happen to us in life.

So if I watch a TV programme about a famine in Africa, I may be moved to donate money because I feel shock or outrage or pity. If someone tells a good joke I will be moved to laugh because I feel amused. That's the link between the words we opened with: our actions and the reasons behind them (motives) are often based on our emotions, the way we feel.

Emotive language, then, means language that tries to stir our feelings so that we will act in a certain way. And although we might link that kind of language with fiction – stories or poems that are exciting or funny or scary etc. – emotive language is also important in many kinds of non-fiction. We might think of the way words are used in adverts and in debates and discussions. But let's think a bit further . . .

If you listen to politicians speak on the news, notice the various ways they try to affect our feelings. And what about how lawyers in the courtroom argue their case to try to prove that the accused is innocent (or guilty)? Although they must work with facts and the evidence, they also use words very cleverly to try and affect the feelings of the jury.

Even in the world of science emotive language is common. When I was a young boy my parents bought me a little book on Astronomy, which opens with the words 'The heavens at night provide one of the most beautiful spectacles in nature. The Moon, the bright planets, the patterns of the stars, are all lovely to look at. . . .' And of course when the words are accompanied by pictures the emotional impact is even greater.

One important way in which language stirs our feelings is by association. That means, a link we make in our mind between one thing and another. Associations can be made quickly and they can be very rich and powerful. And of course it's not only words that can carry associations for us, but pictures, sounds, smells, tastes and textures too. In fact any and all of our senses can trigger associations.

When words try to affect how we feel, it's useful to notice *what's going on in our minds* as we have those feelings. When I watched the news item on TV about the famine in Africa, I was looking at pictures of starving people of course, but I was also thinking about the meal I'd just eaten for tea, and then about how I could also pop down to the supermarket if I felt peckish – I had a picture of the supermarket in my head at that point. Then other thoughts linked up with the ones I'd just had to form a kind of web, and it was this that stirred me to donate some money.

Try making an association web for yourself. Put the word 'golden' in the middle of a large sheet of paper and then add further words to the web, just as the ideas come to you. See how big you can make the web. This is a useful way to explore how emotive language can influence you.

Section 4
Persuasive writing

Language and feelings

The term 'emotive language' usually applies to fiction and the use of persuasive techniques in non-fictional forms, such as advertisements and newspaper articles. However, I think it's worth bearing in mind that, unless we are perhaps dealing with logical arguments structured with a high degree of formality, it's difficult *not* to respond to language with at least some degree of emotional involvement. For instance, the fact that this paragraph is written in the first person (rather than in an impersonal style) and uses the more informal 'it's' rather than 'it is' influences the emotional tone of the writing and thus the way the reader responds. Such features can be subtle and easily missed, but are worth bearing in mind and even pointing out to the children after they have been introduced to some of the more obvious 'tricks' of emotive language.

One way of developing children's awareness of and sensitivity to emotive language – including not just the linguistic techniques themselves but also the nature and degree of the children's responses – is to practise simple exercises in metacognition with the class. Metacognition can be defined as 'thinking about the thinking you do'. But in order to reflect on thinking one must notice those thoughts in the first place. (For more details on developing metacognition see, for instance, my *100+ Ideas* books and *Jumpstart! Creativity*, referenced in the Bibliography.)

All language must be conceptualised in order for a response (emotive or otherwise) to be made. Words trigger thoughts, of course, which may be predominantly visual, auditory, kinaesthetic (tactile) or a more balanced mixture of these. Encouraging children to become more aware of how they think – in this case which sensory mode(s) they tend to use – helps them to gain insight into the emotional response they make to language.

So as children read text ask them to be aware of what they picture in their mind's eye, or what they imagine the writer's tone of voice to be. Often a visual and auditory impression will occur simultaneously. Using more overtly emotive extracts such as newspaper headlines or text from adverts makes the activity easier; you can then progress to more subtle examples later on. Coincidentally, just before writing this page I saw a headline in a tabloid newspaper that said something like 'Now the Government makes it even HARDER to sell your home.'

Even before beginning to notice the techniques that went into the crafting of the sentence I was aware of a sense of outrage and exasperation in the words, as I imagined a stereotypical florid-faced colonel spluttering his disapproval. Now just why that impression came to mind I'm not sure, but the point is (1) the impression happened *quickly* and (2) it supported the emotional tone of the words and hence my first reaction to them.

As you practise this activity with the class, it's worth making clear that there is no single 'right' way of responding to language as far as metacognition is concerned. By that I mean that, while I imagined a ruddy-cheeked colonel in order to respond to the headline, someone else might have pictured a waspish, middle-aged spinster, or a sulky teenager (did you imagine a boy or a girl then?), or whatever. Impressions tend to be individual even when a number of people respond to a piece of language in the same way.

Language with feeling

By 'putting feelings' into your writing I mean writing in such a way that your reader will have emotions as well as thoughts as he or she reads your words. But why bother to try and do that – isn't it enough for your reader simply to understand what you have written? Why do you think stirring your reader's feelings might be useful?

Maybe you agree with me that feelings can influence people even more than reasons can. If I want to persuade you to think or act in a certain way, drawing out your feelings will make my reasons or arguments more powerful – remember what we said about the link between motivation and emotions (see **Module 19**)? That's why you'll usually find what's called *emotive language* in advertisements and newspapers, where the writers want you to buy something or agree with their viewpoint.

Activity: Emotive language

We'll look at this more closely later, but for now let's begin to think about how you can write emotive language. I saw this headline in a newspaper:

> *Now the Government makes it even HARDER to sell your home.*

What feelings do you think the writer wants you to have as you read this? How do you think the writer tried to achieve this? Here are some of my thoughts . . .

- The word 'now' suggests that there have been other times when the Government has made things harder for you.
- The word 'even' suggests that the Government is already somehow making things hard for you, or that it's hard anyway to sell your house.
- 'HARDER' written in capitals means the word catches your eye. Perhaps as you glance at the newspaper it's the first word you see. A word written in capitals is also like shouting (which is why it's bad manners to write in capitals in an email or blog).
- The word 'your' makes it personal. The headline is speaking to you directly. Notice the difference if the headline had said 'Now the Government makes it even HARDER for houses to be sold.'
- And there's even more difference in 'The Government makes it harder for houses to be sold'. Notice how this version doesn't have as much 'punch'.

These are little tricks, but together they can have a powerful effect. Take a look at a few more newspaper articles and adverts to spot other ways of putting feelings into writing. You may have noticed some of the following:

- The use of 'dramatic' verbs and adjectives: 'Unemployment *soars*' instead of 'Unemployment rises' or 'Soldiers *slain* in *bloody* battle' instead of 'Soldiers die in battle'.
- Compare your feelings in this second example with 'Our brave boys slain in bloody battle far from home!' Notice that it's personal ('our'). Notice the alliteration of 'brave boys' and 'far from home', which helps the words to stick in the memory. This phrase also tries to 'tug at your heart strings' by suggesting loneliness and isolation.
- Feelings actually named and described in the writing. 'Loved ones tell of their *anguish* as our brave boys are slain. . . .'
- Quotes from people who talk about how they feel.
- Use of exclamation marks, capitals and bold type to make words stand out.
- 'What if' suggestions. 'It's Christmas Day and you've just opened your brand new ZX64 Ultra Games Console. Happy or what?'
- The use of pictures to support the text.

And that's just for starters! Take a look at **Punchy words** (**Module 17**) or **Hurry while stocks last!** (**Module 16**), if you want to learn more.

Punchy words

The word *influence* means 'to affect or have power over' someone or something. As we've seen, language is often used to try to influence people to think, feel and act in particular ways. As you learn more about this topic, not only will your own language become more powerful (influential), but it's likely that *you won't be so easily influenced by what other people say or write* – because you can see what they're up to. In other words, you'll be able to make up your own mind in a more independent way.

Activity: Punchy words

Here are some ways of making your words more influential:

- Control the way the reader looks at the subject.

  Notice the difference between these two sentences:

  - More than 1,900 people flocked to the concert.
  - Fewer than 2,000 people turned up at the concert.

  Which sentence is trying to make you think that the concert was well attended? How does the writer try to do this? (Tip: we can call this the 'is the glass half full or half empty?' principle.)

- Use questions that the reader can easily agree to.

  For example:

  - Wouldn't you like to live in a country where people are happier, healthier and more contented?
  - Don't you think it's reasonable to want to earn a good living?
  - Do you ever feel that society's problems aren't being dealt with properly?

  (Tip: people trying to sell you things often use the trick of asking three questions that you can say *yes* to, then say something like 'If you could buy a product that would let you have all of that, would you be interested?' Because you've already said yes three times, it's more likely you'll say yes again now.)

- Use strong action words.

  'Strong' in this sense means words that have more of an impact or punch, and can be verbs (doing words), adjectives (describing words) and adverbs (words that describe or add-to verbs). Look back at the two statements that talked

about people going to a concert. The first said that people 'flocked to' the concert and the second said that people 'turned up' at the concert. Which phrase do you think is stronger, and why?

Strong verbs are often action-packed. Which verb do you think is stronger in each of the following pairs – broke/smashed, fell/collapsed, shouted/yelled, threw/hurled?

Strong adjectives and adverbs can appeal to the senses or feelings or suggest that one thing is better or more than another. Sometimes such adjectives exaggerate or 'magnify' the description beyond the truth. For example:

- It was a tasty meal/It was a mouth-watering meal.
- The joke was funny/the joke was hilarious.
- John felt nervous/John felt terrified.
- It was an enjoyable evening/It was a perfect evening.
- Ann replied irritably/Ann replied furiously.

▶ Create a sense of urgency or a feeling that 'time is short'.

Notice how this trick is often used in adverts. Hurry – buy now while stocks last! Take advantage of this offer at once! Global warming will accelerate and problems will increase rapidly unless we do something quickly!

▶ Appeal to the imagination.

In other words, get the reader to picture and anticipate how things can be, for example:

- Can you imagine being happy, wealthy and successful?
- Just pretend for a moment that you've already got everything you ever wanted. What does that feel like right now?
- Suppose you bought our product. Just picture how many ways that will make your life better!

Another trick for influencing people is called *false choice*. But more of that later. Right now, would you prefer to look more closely at how advertisements work (**Module 16**) or move straight on to see how to prepare a good argument (**Module 15**)? The choice is yours – but hurry!

FOR THE TEACHER

Module 16

Hurry while stocks last!

Advertisements are a sophisticated combination of words and pictures (and in TV adverts, sound and movement) that according to some authorities are powerful because they operate partly at a subconscious level. For example, in an essay called 'The language of advertising claims' (see Bibliography), author Jeffrey Schrank suggests that adverts work even for (or against?) those who claim 'immunity to their message'. Schrank goes on to assert that analysing advertising techniques is useful because people unaware of their influence are precisely the ones who are 'most defenceless against the adwriter's attack'.

Above and beyond that, exploring how advertisements work has spinoff benefits for children insofar as such analysis develops observational skills, understanding of language and graphic design, and speaking and listening skills. With older children discussion of the psychological aspects of advertising will be useful; for instance, the psychological associations of colour and how the human face and form are used as 'persuaders'.

Perhaps the first and most important message to children is that in advertising *everything is deliberate*. Every feature of an advert will have been carefully designed with the primary aim of selling the product. So basic questions children can ask as they look at adverts are:

- How is the advert put together?
- Why is each element the way it is?

You may want to explore aspects of advertising that go beyond the scope of this book; our concern here is specifically with the way words are used to influence the reader. As such you can encourage the children to look at some or all of the following:

- the use of adjectives and verbs;
- word associations (making word webs is a useful activity here);
- alliteration and other 'sound effects';
- brand names and slogans;
- word-combos, invented words and catchy phrases.

FOR THE TEACHER

An oft-quoted survey by the linguist Geoffrey Leech (see Bibliography) flags up the adjectives and verbs used most frequently in advertisements (at the time of the survey anyway – it would be interesting to see if the results are the same in a more up-to-date sample); see Table 4. Ask children to make their own lists by looking at adverts in magazines or on TV. Compare these with Leech's findings and then have children use the words in their own invented catchphrases, slogans and invented brand names.

Table 4 Twenty most frequently used adjectives and verbs in advertisements

Adjectives		**Verbs**	
1	new	1	make
2	good/better/best	2	get
3	free	3	give
4	fresh	4	have
5	delicious	5	see
6	full	6	buy
6	sure	7	come
8	clean	8	go
9	wonderful	9	know
10	special	10	keep
11	crisp	11	look
12	fine	12	need
13	big	13	love
14	great	14	use
15	real	15	feel
16	easy	15	like
16	bright	17	choose
18	extra	18	take
18	safe	19	start
20	rich	20	taste

Note: According to Leech these are the most frequently used terms *in order*.

FOR THE TEACHER

Another project is to look at the different kinds of 'power' that adverts represent as they try to influence us. According to the aptly named Peter Sells (Professor of Linguistics at Stanford University) adverts try to persuade us through:

- **Reward power**, which promises a positive benefit.
- **Coercive power**, which contains an overt or implicit threat; an 'or else' message if you don't buy the product.
- **Referent power**, where the product is associated with the target audience's value system.
- **Expert power**, where an expert or authority is used to back up the advertisement's claims. Using celebrities for the same purpose also comes into this category.

When I present these ideas to children I label the power categories promises/threats/values/experts. In one school I visited a Y6 boy nodded his head knowingly as I talked about these things and said 'Oh, our teacher uses most of these too, to get us to behave.'

Hurry while stocks last!

Advertisements (or adverts or ads) are everywhere these days. There are thousands of different ones, put together by very skilled people. But they all have one thing in common – to get you to buy or do something. Even adverts for charities and political parties etc. are trying to persuade you to 'buy into' their beliefs and values. In other words, all ads are trying to influence the way you think, feel and act.

The word itself – advertisement – comes from the Latin *ad+vertere*. 'Ad' means 'towards' and 'vertere' means 'to turn'. So the word means 'to turn towards'. Can you see why that fits in with what adverts are trying to do?

Your teacher may want you to look at the images in adverts as well as the way words are used in them. My job here is to help you to look especially at the language used in advertising.

Activity: Advertising

Let's start with a little experiment. Work with several friends and get them to write down or draw the first thoughts that come into their minds when you say the word 'sweets'. Now do these things:

- If they thought of particular sweets, ask them to think about why that brand of sweet flashed into mind so quickly. To do this they will need to remember what went on in their heads when you said 'sweets'. Did they imagine pictures, hear sounds, remember tastes etc.?
- Force yourself to go to the sweet counter at the shop. Look at several different brands and notice the words on the packets used to advertise them. Make a list.
- Words tend to make links in your mind with other words, pictures, ideas, memories . . . These are called *associations*. Take the word 'golden' and make an association web, like the one you perhaps did in **Module 19**. What kinds of products could you advertise by including the word golden or associated words?

FOR THE PUPIL

Here are a few more projects you can do:

- **Fonts**. The word 'font' in this case means the style of lettering used. When you write using computers you usually have lots of fonts to choose from. Answer the following questions:
  - This font is called Comic Sans MS. How would you describe the style of lettering? Some of the ideas kids have given me include warm, friendly, jokey, cosy, informal. What kind of product would you advertise using this font?
  - This font is called Chasm. What products would you advertise with it and why?
  - This font is Ancestry SF. How would you describe it? Would you use it to sell a) soap powder b) jewellery or c) chocolate? Give a reason for your answer.

- **Slogans**. The word 'slogan' originally meant a battle cry! How do you think that is linked with the way the word is used today, as a catchy phrase in advertisements? Have a look for some slogans, then choose a few different products and invent slogans for them. (Tip: try using *alliteration* to help you.)

- The words in adverts try and trick you in various ways. Look at the examples below and try to find claims that are similar.
  - **Weasel words**. These are claims that seem to be true, but when you look at them more closely they are almost meaningless. One example is 'Hubbly Bubbly Shampoo helps to control dandruff'. The weasel word here is *helps*. Notice that the advert doesn't claim the shampoo stops dandruff. Another example is 'New Slap-It-On Face Cream hides the signs of ageing'. What's the weasel word here?
  - **The unfinished promise**. Here the advertiser starts to compare the product with something else but never quite finishes. 'Snugglies are more than just comfortable . . .' (so what are they?); 'You can be sure with Smiley Toothpaste!' (sure of what?); 'Brussels Sprouts Are Better For You!' (better than what?).

- **The numbers game claim**. Here the advert tries to persuade you with percentages and statistics. Ask your teacher to help you figure out (get it?) how these numbers are trying to trick you. 'Nine out of ten women prefer Lippo Lip Gloss'; 'Crunchyflakes give you 33% more goodness' (notice that this is also an

unfinished promise); 'New Gluggit sports drink makes you healthier in up to six different ways!'

Although this is the end of the block of modules called **Persuasive writing**, you'll find plenty more tricks of persuasion in the next block, which deals with how to write a good argument – Oh no I won't! OH YES YOU WILL!!

Section 5
Writing an argument (discursive writing)

Oh yes it is! Oh no it isn't!

For the purposes of this form of non-fiction writing a distinction is often made between balanced/reasoned arguments and one-sided/persuasive arguments. This can be a simplistic way of looking at things, insofar as even supposedly balanced arguments can be biased, and cleverly reasoned points used to persuade the reader (or listener) to change his or her mind.

The advice given to pupils in this module focuses more on constructing a balanced argument. One reason for dealing with this form first is that it encourages pupils to look at opposing or different viewpoints, and to acknowledge that these can be as relevant as one's own stance, and of course just as strongly felt. I've found that a very useful and powerful workshop is to choose a topic for discussion/debate and ask children to decide on where they stand with the issue. Have them jot down their reasoning. Then invite them to debate the issue, *but taking their opponent's viewpoint*. And, depending on the pupils' capability, ask them to construct extra reasons to support the statements they make.

Another effective technique is to teach the pupils 'Meta-model questioning' (see the teacher's notes for **Types of question** (**Module 27**)). Such questions attempt to elicit precise details or further information from one's opponent and contain words and phrases such as exactly/precisely/in more detail/explain further/other examples of/what in particular, etc. So with regard to the list of statements below pertaining to the issue of car parking charges (also see website materials for an extension of the activity), examples of Meta-model questions are:

(b) *Rail commuters and workers in town will find free parking in side streets rather than pay hundreds of pounds a year to park 'officially'* – Exactly which rail commuters/workers in town do you mean? (Another tactic here is to question the generalisation on which the assertion is made . . . '*All* rail commuters and workers in town?' and 'How exactly do you know that?'.)

(c) *Cases of childhood asthma have increased alarmingly since 1980* – How exactly are you connecting cases of childhood asthma with the car parking charges argument? Tell me more about the evidence suggesting that childhood asthma is linked to traffic pollution. Who exactly is it that finds the increase in asthma cases 'alarming'? 'Alarming' compared to what, precisely?

(i) *Over the past decade motoring costs in 'real terms' have gone down, while travelling by public transport has become more expensive* – Precisely which motoring costs are you referring to? What exactly do you mean by 'real terms'? Which particular forms of public transport have become more expensive? And explain in more detail in what ways different kinds of journeys by public transport (peak/off-peak fares etc.) might have become more expensive? Also, how precisely are you measuring 'more expensive'?

Meta-model questions in verbal discussions should never be asked aggressively or sarcastically. Indeed, they can indicate a respect for the questionee's viewpoint, insofar as the questioner wants to find out more and is interested in what supports or lies behind his or her opponent's stance. When children become more familiar with the technique they can use Meta-model questions as a powerful analytical tool in helping to assess the validity of a written argument.

Oh yes it is! Oh no it isn't!

I had an argument with my wife the other day. I put a chicken leg out on a plate in the kitchen for my lunch, then went to make a phone call before coming back to prepare some salad. The chicken leg was gone! My wife came in from the garden and I said 'Have you eaten my chicken leg?' She said 'No.' I said 'You must have done because it's not there now.' She said 'Well I haven't touched it. Maybe you ate it last night!' I said 'Don't be daft, *I just put it out on the plate*!' She said 'Well I haven't taken it!' I said 'Yes you did!' She said 'No I didn't!' I said 'Yes you did!!' She said . . .

Well anyway it turned out that the cat had taken it, because we found him (Leo the cat) eating it behind the sofa in the lounge.

Most of us will probably have had an argument like that – not necessarily about a chicken leg of course, but the kind of argument I call 'bad-tempered ping-pong'. In that game people throw accusations at each other and just get more and more cross and frustrated. That's not really the kind of argument I'm talking about here.

Interestingly the word 'argue' comes from French and Latin meaning 'to accuse, to reason' and 'to make clear'. In turn, 'accuse' comes from the Latin 'to call to account'. If we put these ideas together we can see that an argument calls for a clear, reasoned exploration and explanation (an account) of an issue that people feel is important. In the true sense of the word it's not a shouting match.

However, there's a bit more – the Latin root of 'argue' also includes the meaning 'noisy' and 'to prate' or chatter. The things people argue about are often those matters that stir up the emotions. Tempers can be lost. And sometimes arguments get personal. It's because of this that people sometimes think they have to win an argument. But is that the best way forward? And can an argument ever be truly won or lost anyway?

If we keep in mind the notion that an argument is an exploration of an issue (an important matter) then the best arguments are:

- clear
- reasoned
- balanced
- thorough.

Somebody once said that a clear voice is more powerful than a loud one, so we can bear this in mind too.

In later modules we'll look at arguments that are one-sided and use plenty of tricks to try and persuade you to agree with the arguer. But for now, let's stick with the rules of thumb above.

Activity: Arguments

I'm sure that you feel strongly about many things:

- Should the Government pass a law insisting on minimum pocket money for all young people at school?
- Should ice cream be free to all children of your age?
- Should younger brothers and sisters do their fair share of household chores? (Actually, they should do all the chores because you're busy eating your free ice cream!)

And I'm sorry if you aren't really bothered about the example I've chosen for us to work with – Should car parking charges be introduced in the town where I live?

You can of course include your own thoughts about this if you want to, but I'd also like you to look at the list of statements below and arrange them in the following way:

1. Separate out statements for and against car parking charges being introduced.
2. In each pile (for/against) decide which statements seem to be facts, which are opinions and which are a mixture of both.
3. Look for any reasons given to support the statements.
4. Question statements that aren't supported by reasons.
5. Decide which statements are very important, which are not so important, and the ones that you think are not important at all. If you can give reasons for your choices, so much the better.

Look at Figure 4. This might help you to organise your thoughts.

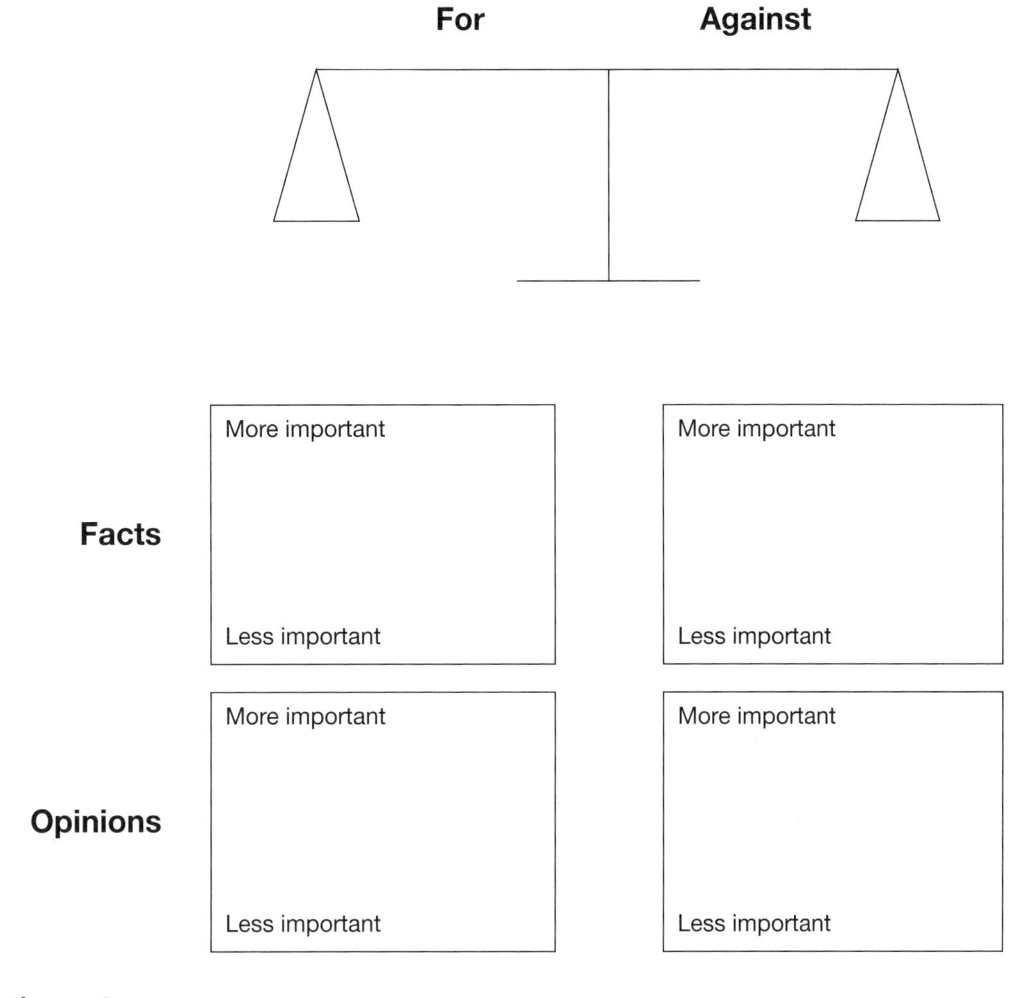

Figure 4

List of statements:

(a) Cars are dangerous and polluting anyway, so why shouldn't they be kept out of town?

(b) Rail commuters and workers in town will find free parking in side streets rather than pay hundreds of pounds a year to park 'officially'.

(c) Cases of childhood asthma have increased alarmingly since 1980.

(d) Education is important. Parents have the right to choose the best schools. Sometimes the best schools are some distance away.

(e) A car-sharing website would be cheap to set up and would save many people plenty of money.

(f) Despite great opposition and lobbying from the public, car parking charges in town are still going ahead.

(g) Market traders now have to pay for their vans to sit outside the Market. Some complain that their profits have been badly hit.

(h) Parents driving their children to their chosen schools sometimes shop nearby for convenience. Car parking charges single out such parents unfairly.

(i) Over the past decade motoring costs in 'real terms' have gone down, while travelling by public transport has become more expensive.

(j) Car parking charges encourage people to use public transport.

Your teacher can give you some tips on how to tackle these statements. Once you've done that, you're ready to plan the argument itself – go to **Module 14**.

Argument planner

The model for structuring an argument in the pupil notes below is one of the simplest and most straightforward. An alternative is to use the 'pyramid planner' (see Figure 5). Here the most basic, obvious or commonplace points are stated first, filling the base layers of the pyramid, followed by logical developments of these points and/or points of greater importance that lead towards the summary and conclusion. A similar template can be used for structuring newspaper articles (see **Module 3**).

With regard to the various arguments for and against a proposition, one way of helping children to reflect on and organise these points is to play 'decision alley'. Write relevant statements related to the issue on separate pieces of paper.

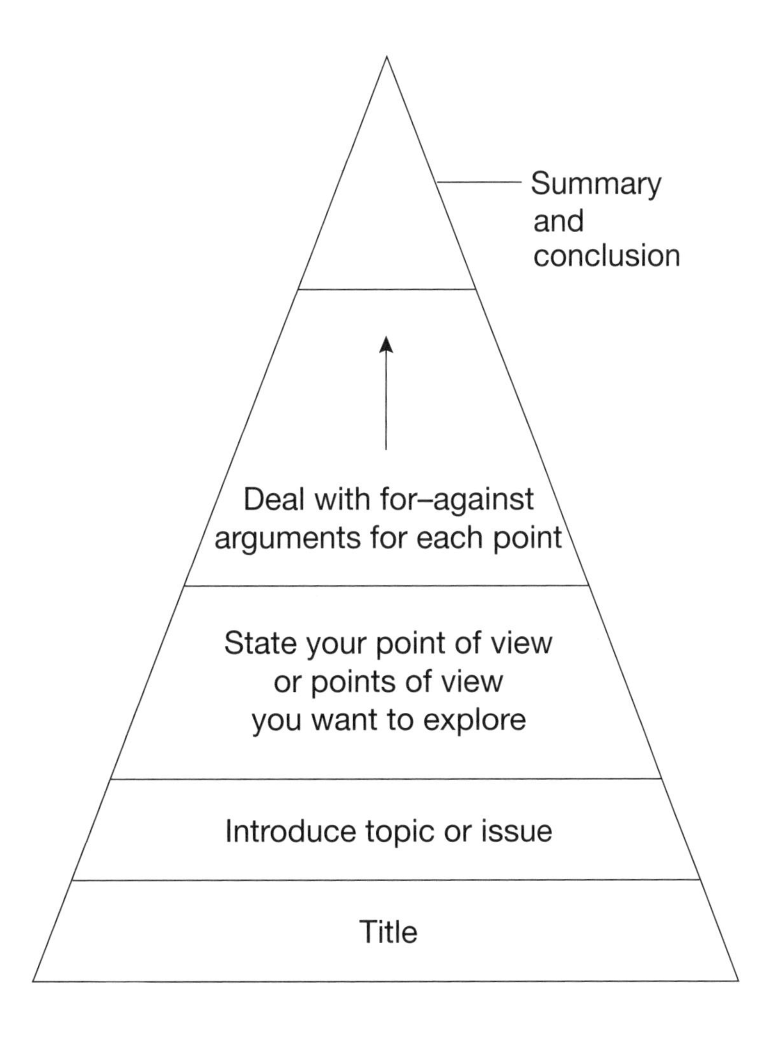

Figure 5

Give one piece to each child. Through their own discussion, children sort themselves out into points for and against. Then, further organise into the least-to-most relevant statements. Have the Fors and Againsts face each other in parallel lines with a walk-space gap between the lines. This is the decision alley.

A small 'neutral' group of children walk slowly one at a time along the alley. As they do, the children forming the alley whisper their points of view. When the neutral group of children emerge, ask them to say if any arguments persuaded them and why.

Finally, in the section below on connectives I make the point that, while connectives might do their job 'grammatically', they don't necessarily ensure that the statements so formed are valid. Pupils are asked to question these statements. Some questions that occurred to me are:

- *As a town council we must introduce car parking charges because the Government has given us less money to spend this year.* Why 'must'? Don't other ways exist of coping with Government funding cuts? And do other councils in the same situation find alternatives to car parking charges? And does the word 'because' mean that the second part of the sentence follows on logically from the first part?
- *Some people have objected to a car parking charge, however many other people support the idea.* What people exactly object to the charges, and for what reasons? What precisely is the difference in number between 'some' and 'many' in your statement? Give further information about why 'many people' support car parking charges.
- *If nothing is done about parking in town, then the situation will only get worse.* What situation do you mean (the Government funding cap)? How sure are you that the situation 'will' get worse? What is your evidence for this assertion? In what way(s) could the situation get worse? And from whose perspective will it 'get worse'? (For example, wouldn't local tradespeople oppose parking charges out of concern that custom will decrease?)

Argument planner

Remember – clear, reasoned, balanced, thorough. In more detail this means:

- **Clear**. Use words that you understand. Don't try to impress people with big words or jargon, or with long, complicated sentences. Make sure your points follow on from one another. Keep your writing plain, simple and straightforward.
- **Reasoned**. Support the points you make with reasons. This will involve using facts – so check they're accurate – and linked statements that are 'reasonable'. By that I mean that the statements make a 'chain of thought' that has been reasoned out. Use connectives to make these chains stronger (I call connectives 'sticky words' – see below). Another feature of a reasoned argument is that what you say is *relevant*. That means keeping to the point.
- **Balanced**. This means understanding both sides of the argument. Even if you feel very strongly about a certain point of view, you must include the opposite point of view too. If you can support your viewpoint through reasoned argument, including opposing arguments can make your position look stronger.
- **Thorough**. In other words, don't gloss over the points you make and look at all sides of the issue if you can. The more thoroughly or completely you explore an issue, the more impressive your piece of work will be.

Sticky words

Maybe you've looked at 'connectives' in school. The job of connectives of course is to connect. That's why I call them 'sticky words', because they stick ideas together and help to turn them into the chains of thought I mentioned above.

Some of the more common connectives that will be of use to us here are – because, therefore, furthermore, however, so, nevertheless, it follows that, alternatively, consequently, if . . . then.

Ask your teacher to help you to understand any of these words that puzzle you. Then try to make some sentences using some of them. Here are a few I did as I thought about the car parking charges issue:

- As a town council we must introduce car parking charges because the Government has given us less money to spend this year.

- Some people have objected to a car parking charge, however many other people support the idea.
- If nothing is done about parking in town, then the situation will only get worse.

Notice that even though connectives 'glue' ideas together in these sentences, the statements themselves can be questioned in various ways. Ask your teacher to show you how. Asking further questions about the ideas in an argument can strengthen your viewpoint and weaken your opponent's (if you're out to win, that is!).

So, planning your argument. By this time you will have:

- looked at points for and against;
- decided which points are facts and which are opinions (some will be a bit of both);
- decided which are the most important points to make;
- looked at ways of helping the points to follow on from one another by using different sticky words.

When you come to write your argument out, one useful plan looks like this:

1 **Title**. This can be a sentence about the issue you are discussing. Or you can think of a short catchy title and state the issue in (2).

2 **Introduce the topic or issue**. State your point of view very briefly – if you have one. You might not have a viewpoint and are using the argument just to explore the topic.

3 **Make the points that support your argument**. Use a paragraph for each point you make and remember also to state the opposing point of view. Some writers prefer to leave the most important points and most powerful reasons till last.

4 **Summarise the arguments**. Write a conclusion presenting the view you agree with/the view that you think is stronger.

(Tip: there are hundreds of issues you can write arguments about. Look at the stories on the TV news or news pages online. Checking out the letters' pages in newspapers will give you plenty of issues to discuss. When you read such letters, you'll see that the writers are usually trying to persuade you to agree with them.) Let's look at persuasive writing now, in **Module 13**.

Persuasive arguments

The word 'persuade' comes from Latin meaning 'to thoroughly advise; urge'. It is the 'urging' association that we most readily think of in connection with the use of persuasive techniques in arguments – the appeal to values and beliefs through the emotions rather than perhaps through reasoned and logical argument. As with many of the techniques and ideas in this book, as children become more familiar with the techniques of persuasion they can use them in their own writing and in analysing the work of others.

Here are some common persuasive devices:

- The use of **persuader words** such as clearly (or clear), surely, undoubtedly, plainly, obviously etc. These can be reinforced by compounding them – 'Surely there can be no doubt that the most obvious reason for . . .?' In this case the persuader words are used within a *rhetorical question*, one that is asked for effect and emotional impact rather than to elicit a considered reply.
- **Emotive language**, which may be combined with generalisations, exaggerated or extreme examples (often in the form of high-impact metaphors) and appeals to the individual. For example:
  - And as a Government we are absolutely steadfast in our war against terror.
  - Over the past ten years the floodgates of illegal immigration have been opened.
  - Have you ever stopped to think how you'd feel if scores of strangers suddenly set up camp in your back yard?
  - Standards in education have never been in greater danger of plummeting.
  - People these days demand the highest levels of professionalism from those in public office.
- **Making it personal**. An attack against an individual or organisation that supports an opposing viewpoint (to that of the attacker) is known as *ad hominem*, literally 'an argument against the man'. Its use is obvious (and odious), although when combined with other persuasive techniques can be very effective.
- **Analogies**. These are metaphors that are often used either to disparage viewpoints, institutions or any kind of opposition to the arguer's case, or to bolster the arguer's thesis. For example:

- The British political system is an outlandish Heath Robinson contraption in dire need of repair.
- The New Literacy Framework is the Eurostar of learning in the twenty-first century.

- ***Ad populum*** is an 'appeal to the people'. The supposition here is that most people want to belong, to have views in common with the majority. Its use in argument sometimes takes the form of an appeal to 'common sense'. The ad populum technique is also used extensively in advertising. For example:
  - Surely we all want our young people to grow up with high moral values and a healthy sense of duty? Bringing back National Service is one clear way of achieving this.
  - Most intelligent parents want toys for their children that are great fun and have high educational value.
- **Appeal to authority**. Citing the claims of experts (sometimes out of context) to support a viewpoint. Again this technique is common in advertising.
- **Appeal to celebrity**. The use of famous people to endorse viewpoints, arguments, products etc.
- **Appeal to cost**. The cost of something is often used as an argument against it. A more insidious influence of this technique is to divert attention away from proper analysis of the figures.
- **Factual inaccuracy/simplistic use of figures, statistics etc**. The hope here is that the readers of the argument won't think to check facts or question statistics, but take them at face value.

Persuasive arguments

The main differences between the kind of argument we have already looked at (a balanced or reasoned argument) and a persuasive argument are that:

- Persuasive arguments usually put only one side of the argument forward. Or, if they put another side forward it's to try and knock it down.
- Persuasive arguments try to appeal more to your feelings.

There are things that we all feel strongly about, even if we don't think of them every day or even very often. But when we get into a discussion about them perhaps we notice our feelings rising? And maybe then there's a temptation to try to convince the other person that we are right?

For me the main value of telling you about persuasive arguments is that *you won't get taken in by them*! This doesn't mean you can't agree with the arguer's viewpoint – just as long as you've accepted it for good reasons.

Basic questions you might want to ask when you read or listen to a persuasive argument are:

- Who is trying to persuade you?
- Why might they want to do that?
- How are they trying to persuade you?
- Are you persuaded? Why/Why not? Because?

Activity: Persuasive arguments

Here's a letter sent to a local newspaper. Can you spot the tricks the writer is using to try to persuade you that he's right?

> Global warming is not my problem!
>
> Sir – Following your article last week on how 'Mankind is responsible for the world heating up', I strongly object to being tarred with the same brush as people who treat their environment like a dustbin! I am always extremely careful to recycle my rubbish and hate to see uncaring slobs dropping litter

on the pavement. Surely it's not too much trouble for them to put their trash where it belongs, in the bin? We are bombarded with stuff on the TV and in the newspapers about keeping our streets tidy and treating our world with respect – don't the eco-vandals who drop litter watch TV? Or is it that they just can't read?

Anyone in their right mind can see that the climate is out of control. More and more experts are telling us that unless we mend our ways now our beautiful Earth is doomed. Clearly we don't want our children to inherit a wilderness. So instead of blaming people like me – people who always try their very best to protect the environment – we should be coming down like a ton of bricks on the ones who really are behind global warming – the drivers of big cars, the thoughtless people who fly off on luxury holidays three times a year, the two-car families, the ones who leave all their electrical equipment on standby . . . The list is endless.

So use your newspaper to get these people to change their minds, and stop blaming me for the catastrophe that's just around the corner!

Albert Hall, Plumstead

As well as picking out the persuasive tricks Albert is using, can you suggest any ways that Albert could make his argument stronger?

Now look at **Module 12** – I'm sure I don't have to persuade you!

Does it follow?

(There are no teacher's notes for this module.)

Arguments are stronger when the points you make follow one another in a reasoned way. One of the weaknesses of Albert Hall's letter in the last module was that he strayed off the point sometimes. Also he didn't always arrange his points so that the one before supported the one following.

Here's what I mean:

- The title of Albert's letter suggests the subject is global warming. However, he doesn't come straight to the point. Instead he talks about people dropping litter.
- In the second paragraph he talks about global warming, but fails to link 'litter droppers', the subject of his first paragraph, with the issue. Instead he targets other groups of people who he feels contribute more than he does to global warming.
- His final paragraph isn't a conclusion to his argument, just a repetition of his anger for being 'blamed' over global warming.

Activity: *Stick to the point*

Now have a go at one of these tasks:

- Using what you have learned about planning an argument, make a plan that discusses the issue of global warming in a more reasoned and balanced way.
- Pretend you are Albert Hall. Rewrite your letter to the newspaper. See if you can get the points you make to follow on more logically one from another. Use as many persuasive tricks as you like to get the reader to agree with you.
- Pretend you are someone who owns at least two big cars, flies away three times a year on holiday and leaves your TV on standby overnight. Write a letter arguing your case – in other words, one that supports your lifestyle.

A note on metaphors

The point of this topic is that metaphors are common in the language and can have a 'hidden influence' on the way we think and feel. My aim is to raise children's awareness of this and to encourage them to question the use of metaphors and begin to 'unpack' the meaning that may lie behind them. Attempting to do this can bring immediate practical results. I once gave a talk on creative writing to a Y5 class, during which the teacher wondered how I overcome writer's block when I hit 'that barrier'. I said 'I put a doorway in it and walk through'. 'Or,' said one pupil, 'you could jump in a hot air balloon and sail over!' This led to a game where we spontaneously created over twenty metaphors that *felt better* than the limiting idea of 'blocks and barriers'.

The emphasis here is the notion that when you change the metaphor you change your (and others') perception of the issue.

More generally, as children develop heightened awareness of the influential nature of language they are more likely to reflect on and question possible intended meanings: they will become more active and creative users of language rather than passive recipients of prepackaged ideas.

These insights are important in the eclectic field of techniques known as Neuro-Linguistic Programming (NLP), which arose in part out of work in General Semantics pioneered by the scientist and philosopher Alfred Korzybski. Korzybski famously said that 'the word is not the thing': all of language is representational (or metaphorical), and practitioners of NLP recognise that we 'filter' meaning during the process of communication, transforming the deep structure of our thoughts – through deletion, distortion and generalisation – into the so-called 'surface structure' of what is actually said. That surface structure is further interpreted by the reader/listener, such that the deep-structure thoughts of the participants will overlap but are very unlikely to correspond exactly, or even closely in many cases. As a past trainer of mine liked to say, 'I am responsible for what I say, but not for what you hear.' Perhaps the most useful lesson we can impart to our pupils is the habit of actively questioning the language to which they are exposed.

Incidentally, an excellent primer on NLP is *Introducing Neuro-Linguistic Programming* by Joseph O'Connor and John Seymour (see Bibliography).

FOR THE PUPIL

A note on metaphors

Maybe you've already looked at metaphors in class? Usually they are taught as one of the figures of speech, along with similes and personification. All of these are kinds of comparison. Your teacher can remind you if your memory of the details is a bit blurred . . .

Hey, did you spot the metaphor there? I said 'if your memory is a bit *blurred*'. When we think of that word we normally think of things being 'out of focus', which is an idea linked with spectacles and lenses. When I talk about a memory being blurred I don't mean it is actually (or literally) so, but metaphorically (or figuratively) so. Another thing people sometimes say if they can't remember or don't know an answer is 'I haven't got the foggiest'. What's the metaphor there – what is being compared to what?

Here's another one – I was watching a cop show on TV and the detective said to a suspicious-looking character 'You just watch your step, Simms. Is that clear?' And Simms said 'Crystal, Gov.' How many metaphors can you track down in that short conversation? (And did you notice that 'track down' is also a metaphor?)

The point I want to make is that metaphors (including similes and personification) are used so commonly that they kind of 'blend in' to the language and become hidden. This is important to us as writers and readers and listeners of non-fiction, because *language has an effect on what we think and how we feel*. And the use of metaphors adds to that influence.

Activity: Metaphors

Have a look at Table 5. The first section lists some of the metaphors that Albert Hall used in his letter to the newspaper in **Module 13**, with a few more for you to think about. There's also space for you to include some metaphors you might hunt down today – There you are, I've let you have the first one free!

* One kid in a lesson told me he didn't think this was a very good metaphor. 'People who throw their rubbish in the dustbin are being clean and tidy and "environmentally friendly"'. He had a point I thought. What do you think?

** If there's ever a word you don't understand, check it out. The Vandals were an East Germanic tribe who destroyed books and works of art in Rome in 455. The word 'vandal' is now used as a metaphor for any deliberate destruction for its own sake. This means that felling a tree that is rotten would not count as vandalism, while felling a healthy tree to build a shopping mall would be. But would felling a tree to build a hospital be called vandalism – what do you think?

Table 5 Exploring metaphors

The metaphor	What was being compared with what?	The meaning without the metaphor
Tarred with the same brush	Albert Hall's reputation with the attitude of people who drop litter	I object to being included in the same group as people who drop litter
People who treat their environment like a dustbin	The environment with a dustbin	*People who throw rubbish away (out of doors/in the countryside)
We are bombarded with stuff on the TV . . .	Advice on keeping streets tidy with bombs dropping from the sky	We are being given advice often about how to care for the environment
Eco-vandals	**People who drop litter etc. with 'vandals' who do other kinds of damage	Don't people who drop litter ever listen to advice about caring for their environment?
The climate is out of control		
Unless we mend our ways		
Earth is doomed		
Coming down like a ton of bricks		
Metaphors you might hunt down		

FOR THE TEACHER

Module 10

Flashpoints

The aim of this module is not to air controversial topics per se, but to alert children to the way in which the strong feelings attached to such subjects can cloud the issue. Evoking powerful emotions can also be used to sway opinion and influence judgement.

When encouraging children to discuss emotionally charged subjects, the *three perceptual positions* ('3PP') technique can prove useful. Arrange three chairs facing each other. Two chairs are occupied by children who hold differing/opposing viewpoints on the matter under discussion. The third chair is for the 'neutral observer', whose job is to listen to points made on either side without judgement, simply noticing the way the arguments are made, then feeding back to the other two participants.

The game can be extended by inviting participants to change chairs (perceptual position) for further discussion, and by having more than one child in each perceptual position.

FOR THE PUPIL

Flashpoints

A 'controversial' issue is one that people usually feel very strongly about. When discussions arise over such an issue emotions can run high. It's easy to take other viewpoints as a personal attack, to feel offended and, in turn, to be aggressive in defending your point of view.

By the way, do you notice the metaphors I'm using to explain this idea? – attack, offended, aggressive, defending. These are words of conflict, of war! Even talking about the *idea* of controversial subjects can get my mind ready for a fight. Good job I noticed what I was saying.

Of course there's nothing wrong with having strong feelings about various issues. You have a right to hold whatever beliefs and opinions you like. However, I reckon it's always worth thinking about why you hold those beliefs so passionately. In my own case, I realise I had strong feelings about some subjects because my parents or friends held the same view and I just wanted to fit in. In other cases, changing my outlook would mean challenging my values in an uncomfortable way, making me admit something that maybe I didn't want to. In yet other cases I just hadn't given the issue much thought.

What this boils down to is that, if you give thought to controversial subjects in a cool, calm and collected way, you are more likely to be in control of your thoughts and feelings, instead of them (and other people) controlling you.

Activity: Controversial issues

In fact, let's use this as a tool, the '3Cs' – being *cool, calm, collected* – when we explore controversial issues:

- ▶ Have a look in some newspapers/on the TV news to see what controversial issues are making the headlines today. You'll have realised that subjects that stir up strong feelings (sex, religion, politics, the rising cost of sweets) make good news stories! Here are some I found on the BBC website (www.bbc.co.uk) on 13 April 2009:
  - Soldiers in Thailand charge on anti-Government protestors.
  - Sir David Attenborough (a famous broadcaster) speaks out about the 'frightening' increase in human population. The Optimum Population Trust, to which Sir David belongs, has launched a *Stop at Two* online pledge encouraging couples to limit the number of children they have.

- Schools are 'employing bouncers' to 'crowd control' classes when teachers are away. (The issues here are (1) whether people not qualified as teachers should supervise classes and (2) whether the 'stern and loud' approach of the 'bouncers' is a positive one.)
- Most Britons 'believe in Heaven'. The survey of 2,060 people showed 55 per cent believe in heaven, while 53 per cent believe in life after death and 70 per cent believe in the human soul.

- ▶ Pick one news story and notice how different newspapers cover it. Ask your teacher about *bias* before you do your comparison.
- ▶ Make a list of four or five subjects that you feel strongly about. Do a survey of your friends to find out what issues are important to them. Compare your viewpoints on a couple of these matters (noticing how you feel as you do this. Remember – *cool, calm, collected*).

The next module suggests some tips on judging the accuracy and usefulness of an argument. Bounce over there now and check it out.

FOR THE TEACHER

Assessing arguments

The notion of assessment isn't used here to help us weigh up how far children have utilised the techniques available for constructing sound arguments (i.e. achieved the learning objectives), but rather to offer a template for helping the pupils themselves to judge the validity and reasonableness of arguments they encounter. However, in becoming incisive evaluators of arguments they are likely to use assessment tools more readily when structuring their own:

- Does the argument follow a logical structure? Is the introduction clear and to the point? Does the author state his or her own point of view in the matter?
- Do points follow on one from another such that the argument 'builds'?
- Is the argument balanced so that contrasting viewpoints are considered fairly?
- Is the summary concise and does it reasonably represent the viewpoint(s) being explored?
- Does the conclusion round off the argument in a satisfying way? If the argument favours one particular point of view, is that conclusion the result of a robust chain of reasoning through the body of the piece? Or is there 'hidden bias' in how points are made?
- Are opinions supported by facts and/or by reasoned exploration of the point raised?
- Are the facts in the argument accurate? Does the author quote her or his source? Was more than one source cited by the author as a way of verifying the facts?
- How is information presented? If charts, tables, figures and diagrams are used, is the presentation clear and does the information support the argument and help the reader's understanding of the issues?
- Are the author's main purposes clear? Is the argument to inform, entertain, persuade, or a mixture of these?
- Are persuasive techniques used? – appeal to authority, appeal to the people, analogies, generalisations etc.? Are these persuaders supported by fact and reasoning?

At the heart of assessing arguments is the attitude of reflective questioning, whereby children are encouraged to ask themselves and others about various facets of the argument.

Assessing arguments

Some years ago I was really into a science fiction programme on TV called *The X-Files*, where agents Mulder and Scully investigated unexplained happenings such as UFOs, ghosts, vampires and so on. Agent Mulder's catchphrase was *Trust No One*!

Well, I'm not suggesting we go that far as we read and listen to other people's arguments. Not everyone is out to deceive us. On the other hand, being a good reader, listener and writer of arguments means not being gullible – in other words, not simply believing what we're told without question.

And that's the key. When we read other people's arguments we can judge how effective they are by asking questions. And when we want to write arguments ourselves, bearing the same questions in mind helps us to make our arguments stronger.

Activity: Assessing arguments

Take a look at Figure 6. I call this the Question Star. When you come across an argument, asking questions under these headings will help you to make sound judgements.

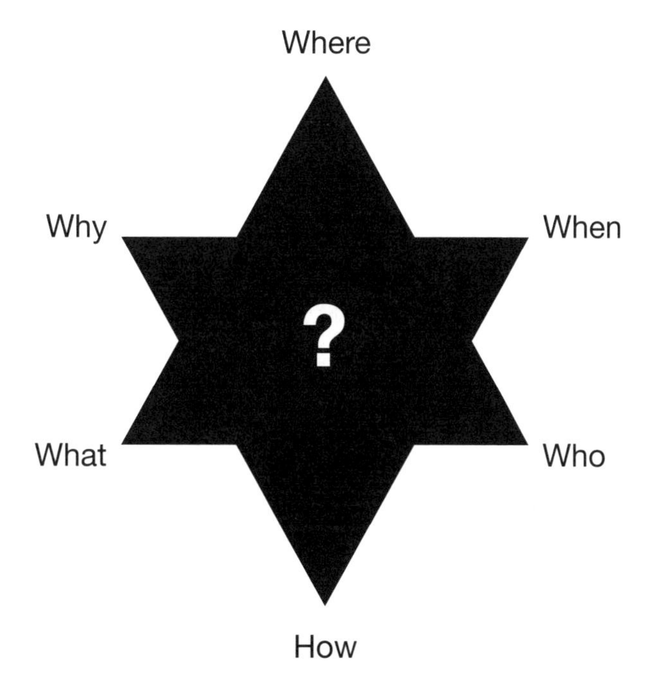

Figure 6

So we could ask questions like:

- Who is the argument mainly aimed at?
- Who is the author and how is he or she qualified to make these points?
- What opinions are being used? How are they supported by facts?
- How is the author trying to persuade me to accept her or his point of view?

Work with your teacher and friends to add more useful questions to the list (not that your teacher isn't also your friend as well, of course!).

Weasel words

These are words and phrases that are often used in arguments. They are often vague in meaning and are not supported by the facts. Weasel words try to trick you in various ways:

- **Vagueness**. 'Scientists have found out that doing less homework makes children more intelligent'. Which scientists? How have they found this out? Which children are they speaking about? How exactly does doing less homework make children more intelligent? What do you mean by the word 'intelligent'?
- **Passive voice** (ask your teacher about this). 'It is said that honesty is the best policy' (rather than 'Steve says that honesty is the best policy'). Who said this? What evidence do they have for saying this? 'Best' compared to what other policies? Is honesty always the best policy?
- **Points not following on** (non sequitur). Note: this can be a tricky one to spot, since sticky words are sometimes used to make the argument more believable. 'Because everyone appreciates a sense of humour, people with a good sense of humour will be more popular.' Why does it follow that if I like a sense of humour I'll like a particular person who has a sense of humour? What is the evidence that 'everyone' appreciates a sense of humour? What is a 'good' sense of humour?
- **The iron fist in a velvet glove**. This is where something unpleasant or offensive is said in a 'softer' or less brutal way. Your teacher will call this trick a *euphemism*. 'Sadly we will have to let staff go. . . .' That means 'fire them'. By the way, who does the word 'sadly' apply to?

A good way to spot weasel words is to check out advertisements on TV and in magazines etc. Also it has been known for politicians to use them in their speeches . . .

FOR THE PUPIL

So why talk about it?

(There are no teacher's notes for this module.)

You probably realise by now that I love words and where they come from. I checked out the word 'discussion' and found that it comes from Latin and means 'to shake apart'! Can you figure out how that definition has anything to do with arguments and debates?

In my opinion, when we discuss ideas we learn more about them very quickly. Speaking about our ideas means that we have to *focus our thoughts*. That's very important. The mind works quickly and can easily jump about all over the place, from thought to thought. If you've ever 'let your imagination run away with you' you'll know what I mean. That's when we snatch at the first thoughts that spring to mind and just string them together. What we end up with if we write them down is a chain of first thoughts rather than a chain of *considered* thoughts. Discussing them to begin with means we consider them before writing them up.

This block of modules has been about writing an argument. Do you remember what we said earlier, about arguments turning into quarrels? Thoughts and feelings go together. 'Maps' of thoughts form our beliefs and what we value in life. Most of us will feel very strongly about some things. Understandably we can get angry if we feel people are being critical. Sometimes they are being critical on purpose, just to be offensive. In my opinion such people are not worth bothering about. But more often, perhaps, people let their own emotions get in the way and don't understand that *a clear voice is better than a loud voice*. So another value of discussion is to learn to be clear rather than loud.

Your rights in a discussion are:

- You have the right to your beliefs. Other people have the right to theirs. You might disagree about things, but the point of discussing ideas is not to 'win' the argument but to learn more about other people's viewpoints – and for them to learn more about yours.
- You have the right to be listened to until you have finished speaking. That applies to everyone in the discussion, of course.
- You have the right to ask questions. The best questions don't try to trick people or catch them out, but to learn more about their ideas.
- You have the right to judge ideas but not people. It's more constructive to say 'I think that idea is mistaken because . . .' rather than to say 'You are wrong' or – even worse – 'That's stupid.'

- You have the right to privacy. If there are personal things you choose not to say, that's fine.
- You have the right to say 'I don't know'. That doesn't make you wrong, it simply means you'd like to learn more.
- You have the right to change your mind. This is not a sign of weakness – instead it's a sign of strength and maturity. If you weigh up the different sides of the argument and come down on a different side, it shows you have an intelligent and grown-up attitude.
- You have the right to leave the discussion before it's over. That's not necessarily running away – you or anyone else might move away from the discussion for any number of reasons. Simply respect their decision and expect them to respect yours.

And respect lies at the heart of all proper discussions. When you hear people quarrelling and name-calling as they talk to each other you know their standards are not as high as yours.

We're ready to start our last block of modules now. Look at **Some tips** (**Module 7**) before choosing another kind of writing to study.

FOR THE PUPIL

Section 6
Writing to inform

Some tips

(There are no teacher's notes for this module.)

This block of modules is about 'writing to inform'. The word is linked to 'information' and it means 'to give shape to'. What we are giving shape to of course is ideas and knowledge, so that people's understanding increases after they've read what we have written.

In order to help other people to gain greater understanding, we must give shape and structure to our informational writing first.

The Big Four tips are:

1 Never write about something that you don't understand yourself.
2 Always do your best to put things into your own words.
3 Keep things as simple as possible.
4 An apple a day keeps the doctor away. (This one's a joke, sorry – although perhaps good advice anyway.)

Tip 1 is really saying that it's pointless to copy other people's work, which includes just downloading stuff from the Internet. If you don't understand something yourself, how do you know it's in the 'best shape' for someone else?

Tip 2 follows on from the first tip. When you try to use your own words to frame ideas, those ideas mean more to you and you understand them better.

Tip 3 is a bit of advice from the great scientist Albert Einstein. I think he might have been talking about physics at the time, but what he says is equally useful when we want to write to inform.

I still think tip 4 is a good one. Do you suppose it works with grapes?

I haven't quite finished yet. Here are a few more pointers:

- Ask yourself often 'Basically what am I trying to say here?' Applying the first three tips above will help you to write clearly, simply and confidently.
- What words best express what you want to say? Usually these are ordinary, everyday words rather than jargon, and shorter rather than long-winded sentences.
- Does the form of the writing suit what you want to say? By that I mean will you give best shape to your ideas through a news article/a list of instructions; using a friendly personal style/a more serious 'formal' style etc.? You can also ask yourself if your work will benefit by you including numbered lists, diagrams, charts, pictures and so on.

Finally, when you've written something try it out on a few people to see if your explanations are clear to them.

OK, let's practise some of this stuff . . .

Descriptive writing

Under the heading 'Hard to teach concepts in English' on the UK Government's Standards website (http://nationalstrategies.standards.dcsf.gov.uk/node/97228), the point is made that many students find descriptive writing difficult to plan because they do not have the skill to visualise what it is they want to write about. This may well be true, although in my opinion we all have the potential to visualise. I qualify the remark, however, by adding that we all represent what we experience in different ways within our imagination – that is we 're-present' the sense we've made of the world naturally though uniquely. One aspect of this ability is the sensory mode or modes we apply to our own imagined worlds, i.e. whether we are more visually oriented thinkers, more auditory, more kinaesthetic or use a more balanced mix of these.

The notion of these and other representational systems is a key feature of Neuro-Linguistic Programming (NLP) mentioned earlier, and is a subject well explained in O'Connor and Seymour's aforementioned book (see Bibliography). Central to developing the ability to visualise using all sensory modes is making children more familiar with noticing and manipulating their own thoughts. This process is called metacognition – 'thinking about thinking'. It is discussed in many books on so-called Accelerated Learning and is a subject I deal with in detail in several of my own books, for instance *ALPS StoryMaker* and *Countdown to Creative Writing* (see Bibliography). A further resource that I've found useful is www.thewritingsite.org/resources/genre/descriptive.asp.

What is important to bear in mind (as it were) is that we all visualise most of the time. We can't help it, it's natural. Helping children to become more metacognitive is simply an extension of what they do anyway. I want to emphasise this because I still come across adults who say of a child or group of children 'Don't expect too much from them. They haven't got any imagination.' Ask just about any child to tell you in some detail about a meal they had yesterday, or to describe a TV show they've watched, or to tell you about what they plan to do at the weekend. To make any response at all the child has to represent the reply within the imagination before 'speaking it out'. This is the resource we work with.

Another point is that visualisation, indeed thought itself, is not a concept but an *experience* – a complex weave of thoughts, emotions and physical sensations. We imagine using all of ourselves, as the anecdote in the pupil's section makes clear. Furthermore, as children become more metacognitive they enjoy increasingly rich experiences as they visualise. Like any skill, the benefits are cumulative.

Descriptive writing

To describe something is to mention certain details of it so that whoever reads or hears the words can imagine it in their own minds. Everybody can imagine and, as with any ability, with practice you get better.

Descriptive language crops up everywhere – it is in fact a very vague term. Descriptions crop up in all kinds of writing, not just the kinds we're looking at in this book, but in fiction – stories and poems – too. There are so many kinds of descriptive writing that part of our skill as writers is to decide which kind or style of description best serves our particular purpose.

Activity: Descriptive writing

Here's a thing – imagine an apple. You probably did it in a second. Now notice how you imagined it. Did you see it? Did you taste it? Did you remember an occasion, such as a picnic, when you ate apples? When you're aware in a bit more detail of the thoughts you had in imagining the apple, you immediately have something to write about.

Here's a story. I was doing some descriptive writing with a class and asked them to write a description of an apple. All the children took up their pencils and started, except for one boy who sat staring at the table for a minute. There was nothing on the table! But then he reached out, picked up an invisible object, looked at it close up, sniffed it, rubbed it on his shirt then took a big bite . . . *Then* he wrote his description of the apple. It was among the best in the class. When I asked him what he'd been doing he said 'Imagining the apple. But your imagination is all over you, isn't it, not just in your head?'

I couldn't agree with him more.

So when you want to describe an object from your imagination – see it, touch it, smell it, hear it, taste it (unless it's a frog). In other words, have the experience yourself before you try to give your reader the experience. Let's make that our first tip:

- Experience what you want to describe with all of your senses.

  The boy's description of the apple was only half a page long. But when I read it my mouth was watering. Even though this young writer hadn't put loads of details in his description, he'd chosen a few powerful details carefully. Next tip . . .

- Choose a small number of vivid details.

  Which details are they going to be? Well, that's for you to decide. You can make your descriptive details more vivid (more 'alive' in the imagination) by using:

  - **strong adjectives** – which are describing words anyway;
  - **verbs** (doing words) with plenty of action in them;
  - **comparisons** such as similes, metaphors and personifications (ask about these if you need to);
  - some **exaggerations**.

  So, for instance, if you're describing people, sometimes you need only drop a sentence or two into the reader's imagination and they'll fill in the rest for themselves. Here are some characters I invented who belong to a group called the Double Dare Gang (DDG):

  - Anthony has sticky-out ears and the skinniest legs I ever saw, but he's the fastest runner in the school.
  - Kevin has a wild look in his eyes and hair that sticks out like a shock of straw. We call him the Mad Professor.
  - Brian is a big square-looking kid with muscly arms like pistons.
  - Neil is shaped like a peardrop. He loves wearing blue.

Did you fill in other details for yourself? Here's another tip . . .

- Use strong language. (No, not *that* kind of strong language!)

Activity: Thumbnail descriptions

Choose a couple of people you know and try doing little 'thumbnail' descriptions like I did above. Remember not to write anything offensive. To do a good job with any kind of description you need to *observe*.

Next tip . . .

- Notice interesting details so that you can put some of them in your descriptions. Finally . . .

- Notice how other writers make what they describe leap out of your imagination. Learn from the masters!

Everything I've said boils down to the big question:

What do you want your reader to experience?

The key word is 'experience'. Don't just tell your reader about something when you describe it. Make your reader imagine it as though it were really there.

Activity: *A short description*

Here are some topics. Choose one and write a short description bearing in mind the tips we've looked at:

- A meal you really enjoyed.
- An exciting action scene from a movie you've watched.
- A person who interests you.
- A famous painting.
- A fascinating or dramatic landscape.

Now it's time to find out if we need to get personal. Leap to **Module 5**.

FOR THE TEACHER

A question of style

These are also known as informal and formal styles. More formal, impersonal writing tends to leave out any reference to the writer, such that the work tends to be more detached and 'distant', and can lend a tone of authority to the words (whether the writer is really authoritative or not!). A formal style is usually adopted for reports, academic pieces, business transactions, legal documents and so on. It also sometimes takes the passive rather than the active voice, for example, *a mistake has been made* rather than *I made a mistake*. The impersonal style generally concerns itself with ideas and 'truths' rather than with individuals.

A personal style is more informal, and 'person-oriented' through the use of personal pronouns and greater use of the first person, which creates a stronger sense of the emotional involvement of the writer with the subject and more warmth between writer and reader.

Some debate does exist about whether a rigid formal style is better suited to academic writing. At worst, impersonal writing can sound pompous and old-fashioned 'in this author's considered view'. Some commentators advise a controlled and minimal use of informal devices when writing pieces that would traditionally fall within the province of the impersonal voice. This is good advice, I feel, especially when we are trying to encourage children to be interested and involved in the writing they do.

A question of style

When you text – sorry, txt – a message to your friends, or if you wrote them a letter, your writing style would probably be chatty and friendly. How would you make it like that? Think about it before reading my ideas below . . .

A chatty written style:

- is more about people;
- uses words like I, we, you, us (personal pronouns);
- shortens phrases to make them sound more informal (i.e. chattier) – so 'I will' becomes 'I'll'; in text messages of course you use even more tricks to shorten words and phrases, ifkwim;
- is more like the way we speak, so it would be OK to write 'OK' – OK?
- would rather say 'We made an arrangement' than 'An arrangement has been made' – this is the difference between what's called the active voice and the passive voice; ask your teacher to tell you more.

This chatty way of writing is also called the informal or personal style. But sometimes when we write we don't want it to sound chatty; it has to sound more 'businesslike' and formal. This style is called – guess what? – the formal or impersonal style. It tends to leave out the things the chatty, personal style would include.

And so the formal style:

- is more about ideas;
- doesn't often use personal pronouns (though sometimes can't avoid it);
- tends not to shorten phrases and words;
- is less like the way we speak (for all the reasons in this list);
- tends to use the passive voice.

Some kinds of writing are a mixture of the formal and informal styles – like this book for instance. The teacher pages are less informal than the pages I've written for you – not that I don't like teachers, you understand!

Activity: Writing style

As you learn more about writing non-fiction you'll see where it's better to use a formal style and where a chattier style is more suitable. For now, have a go at one of these short tasks:

- Find an example of a formal piece of writing and an informal piece. Notice how the writers create those different styles.
- As a class project, make a list of where you would find the formal writing style – for example in a textbook, in a business contract etc.
- Pretend you are a bank manager or a solicitor or someone 'official'. Write a short formal letter to a client or customer that begins 'It has come to our attention that . . .'. Decide on the point of the letter before you begin. If you need a few tips on letter writing go to **Module 2**.

OK (said Steve chattily) time to move on. You can choose **Directions and instructions** (**Module 4**), **Recounting and reporting** (**Module 3**) or **Writing a letter** (**Module 2**) – unless your teacher tells you otherwise.

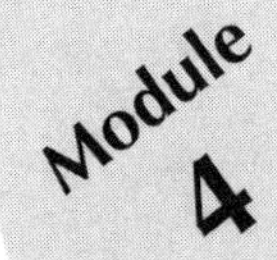

FOR THE PUPIL

Directions and instructions

(There are no teacher's notes for this module.)

If someone asked you directions to a certain place in town, you'd probably use a friendly, chatty style when you spoke to them (see **Module 5**). If that same person used a SatNav, the voice would tend to speak more formally and impersonally. But in either case those directions would have to be:

- clear
- to the point
- sequenced.

Directions like these are a particular kind of instruction. That word – instruction – comes from Latin and means 'to build' (have you noticed how it's a bit like 'structure'?). And what we build when we give or receive instructions is a clearer idea of how to do something.

When you are writing instructions, as well as bearing the three points above in mind you will also need to include:

- a title for your writing;
- (perhaps) a list of equipment, ingredients etc.;
- (perhaps) diagrams, pictures etc.

There are loads of activities you can try out to practise instructional writing. (Your teacher might be interested in this website: www.primaryresources.co.uk/english/englishD2.htm.)

Activities: Instructional activities

Here are a few that I enjoy:

- Hide an object (a book, a tennis ball etc.) somewhere in your classroom. Pretend that I have to find it, never having visited your school before. Write some instructions directing me from the staff car park to the hidden object. Remember, I don't know anybody's name and I don't know my way around – so you can't say 'It's hidden under Miss Roberts' copy of *Gossip* magazine in Room 2.'

- Look at the map in Figure 7. This is a town I made up for some stories I wrote about a group of friends – Anthony, Kevin, Brian and Neil. You might remember them from **Module 6**?
  - Add more details to the map, such as street names, various buildings, features in the landscape.
  - Your starting point is Kenniston High School. Pick a destination somewhere in town and (1) direct someone there using a chatty, friendly style, then (2) pretend you're a SatNav voice and direct someone there using a more formal, impersonal style.
- Here are some directions I gave leading from the High School first to Kev's house and then on to the garages up near the waste ground. I didn't do it very well, as you see. Your job is either to write them properly (adding street names as you wish) or to comment on why my directions are not very good:

  OK, right well – um, come out of the school gates and cross the road. You'll see the supermarket. Go past that and then keep walking for a while. After a while you can turn left towards the park but before then there's a street – it's a cul-de-sac – and at the bottom is Kev's house.

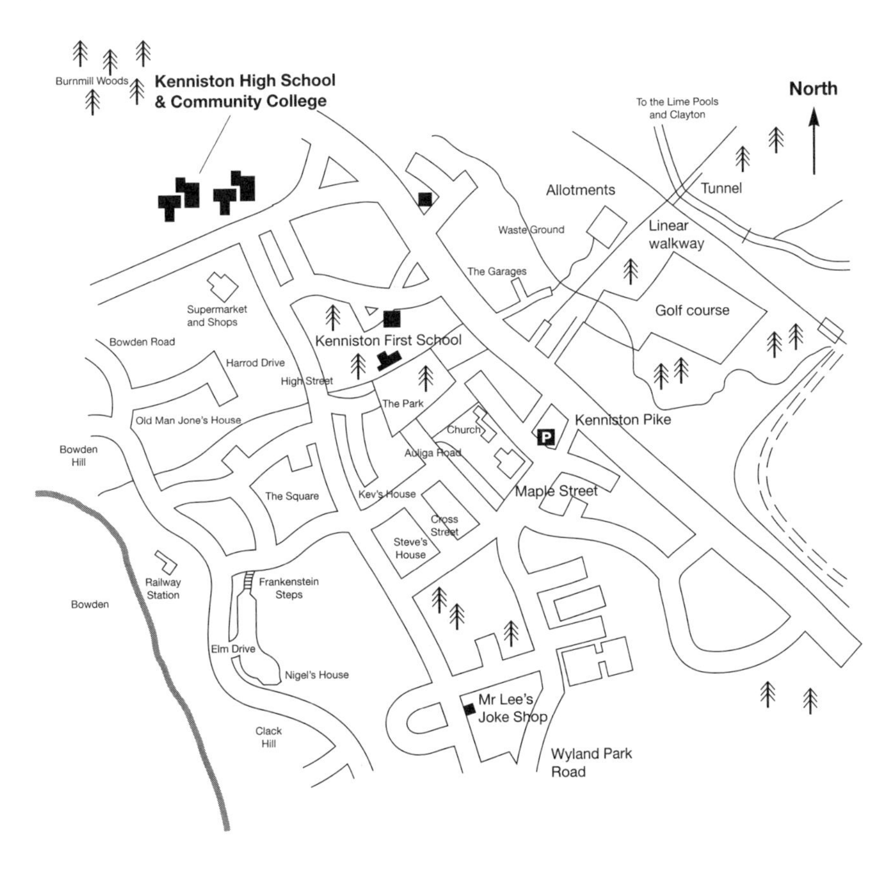

Figure 7

When you've been to Kev's walk back up the street then get to the High Street. Turn left and go down as though you were going to Steve's house – but you don't go there, you need to keep going down the High street until you get to Maple Street then go along Maple Street until you reach the Kenniston Pike. Then turn left and you'll see the golf course go past that and the linear walkway (route of the old railway line) and soon after on the right you'll be near the garages. Hope you don't get lost. . . .

- Play Artist and Instructor. This is a game for a group or the whole class:
  1. The instructor decides on an object to describe. Either write down the name of the object or use a picture. *Do not show this to anyone!*
  2. Somebody from the group/class volunteers to be the artist. The artist stands by the white board and gets ready to draw.
  3. The instructor begins to describe the object one line at a time. You are not allowed to use the names of parts. So if we used the example of the helicopter in Figure 8, the instructor could not say 'rotors' or 'cabin', but would begin something like this . . .

Draw a large circle.

Now draw a short, slightly curved line coming out from the bottom of the circle.

Now draw a horizontal (lying flat) line so that the vertical line touches it about halfway along.

Until you've got . . .

This game is not as easy as it seems!

Figure 8

Recounting and reporting

Recounting, or retelling, is one of the most common text forms and bridges the gap between fictional and non-fictional areas of writing. Such a broadly applicable form is also used therefore both to entertain and to inform.

Although recounting has been judged as one of the easier written forms to master, helping children to write effective narratives, for example, is an ongoing issue in primary education, while oral recounting (either of factual events or storytelling) demands a set of communication skills that seem not to be widely taught. So for me the claim is contentious.

However, recounts (sometimes called accounts) embody a robust yet quite simple structure that can be summed up as:

- orientation or setting the scene;
- a sequence of events, which is largely but not entirely in chronological order – flashbacks and the use of connective words and phrases such as 'meanwhile' and 'but before that' give flexibility to the structure;
- 'reorientation' in the form of a closing statement or 'rounding off' the narrative.

Usually recounts are written in the past tense, feature a personal/informal style, focus on individuals and use more or fewer 'dramatic devices' depending upon the context of the retelling. A personal anecdote of some exciting incident might employ many of the features of good storytelling – emotive language, exaggeration, vivid similes and metaphors etc. However, a witness statement to the police would (probably) leave much of this out and try to stick to the plain facts.

Reporting, as in a news article, is a written form usually included under the umbrella of recounting. Here will be found the basic structure of a recount, but often together with fragments of personal anecdote, opinion, editorial comment etc. Sometimes the political bias of the newspaper colours the plain telling of the story.

There is wide recognition that, because most children love to tell stories, cultivating this interest offers a natural lead-in to developing the skills of recounting – and beyond that to the web of communication skills mentioned earlier. Plenty of oral work, modelling the skills of storytelling and exposure to various kinds of stories prepare the ground for the more formal teaching of written recounting and reporting.

Recounting and reporting

Whenever I visit schools I like to wear a cool tie. One of my best has got the TARDIS on it. Another favorite has pictures of Elvis (and if you have to ask 'Who is Elvis?' I will be very disappointed!). My fondness for colourful ties started some years ago when I visited a school wearing a plain blue tie – the school wasn't wearing the tie, I was, you understand.

Anyway, there I was in the hall talking to the children and at one point I said 'Do you have any questions about what it's like to be an author and write books?' Lots of hands went up, but one boy at the back scrambled up off the floor and was waving his arms to attract my attention. I said 'Hey, before you fall down and hurt yourself what do you want to ask me?' He said, 'I don't want to ask you anything I want to *tell* you something.' So I said, 'OK, what do you want to tell me?' And he said, 'That tie you're wearing – it's a really *sad* tie!'

Well I realised he was right of course and that's when I decided to get some really cool ties . . .

That little incident really happened and I'm telling it to you now. Actually I'm *re*telling it because I've told it before to other people. Retelling is also called recounting, and included with that is reporting, which is a kind of recounting you normally find in newspapers.

Your teacher will tell you more about how to write recounts. But, before that, notice some of the features of my story. Here are the main ones:

- It's mainly about people.
- It's written in the past tense.
- It's informal in style (see **Module 5**).
- It tries to get you to imagine the scene vividly.
- It sets the scene straightaway, gives you a little chain of events (what the boy and I said to one another), and then rounds off the story with a punchline and mentioning again the subject of the story – my cool ties!

Stories like this (and fictional stories too) can be colourful and funny (or scary, or dramatic etc.). Other kinds of retellings have to be simple recounts of the facts, for example if you witnessed a road accident and had to describe what happened to the police.

Activities: Recounting

Being able to recount in these different ways is an important skill to master, I think. Here are a few tips and activities to help you on your way . . .

Story Strips

1 For this game you'll need to make two sets of cards. On one set draw some simple pictures (or get them from magazines, or use clipart). You'll be using these pictures to make up a story. Keep them face up so you can see them all.

2 On the other set of cards write down different connective words and phrases, such as 'meanwhile', 'later on', 'an hour before this', 'three miles away' – and so on. Your teacher will help you to do this. Turn the connective cards face down.

3 Now take some of the little pictures – five or six will do – and arrange them in a line, but with gaps between (see Figure 9a).

4 Chat with your friends about what the story could basically be about; just a short outline will do.

5 Turn up the connective cards one at a time, placing a card in each of the gaps between the story (see Figure 9b).

6 Now retell the story (changing it if you have to) so that you use most or all of the connective words in the recounting.

Note to the teacher: You can find out more about this technique in my *Jumpstart! Creativity* (section on Prediction Strips; see Bibliography).

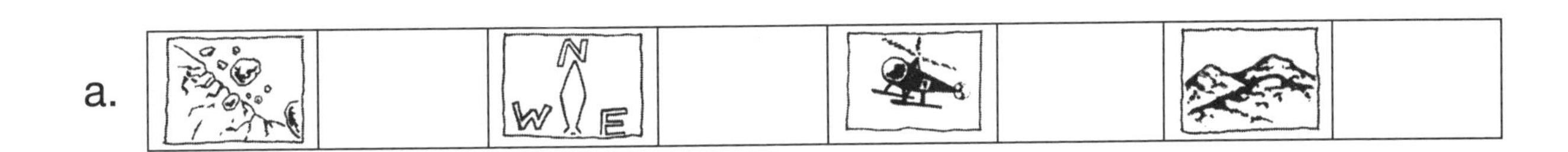

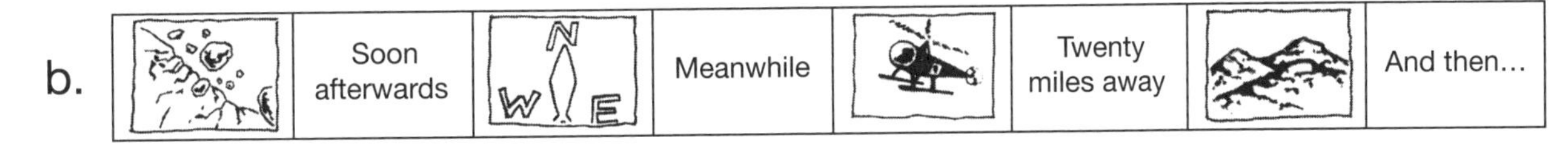

Figure 9

Game of Clues

1 Imagine a crime happening. Make up a short story of the events.

2 Now make a list of clues that a detective would notice when he or she comes to investigate the scene later.

3 Write down the list of clues and pass them on to another group. You of course will get someone else's list of clues.

4 Using your new set of clues (from another group), decide what could have happened.

5 Imagine you witnessed some or all of the events. Write a short witness statement giving the plan facts of what you saw/heard.

If you want a quick practice of this, read my list of clues below. Decide what might have happened and make your witness statement:

- There is a shoeprint in the flower border outside the kitchen window.
- The kitchen window is partly open.
- There is a smashed plate on the kitchen floor.
- A small wooden box on the side table in the lounge has been left open.
- There is mud on the lounge carpet.
- There are no umbrellas in the umbrella stand in the hallway.

If you want more of a challenge, think of three different stories that could explain these clues.

If you want even *more* of a challenge, pretend you are the detective on the case. Make a list of ten questions that you could ask the witness about what he or she saw. (Note: You don't have to know the answers!)

Newspaper Article

Figure 10 shows you how a newspaper article is structured. If you've done the Game of Clues activity, use the template and write up a short news article reporting the event for the local paper.

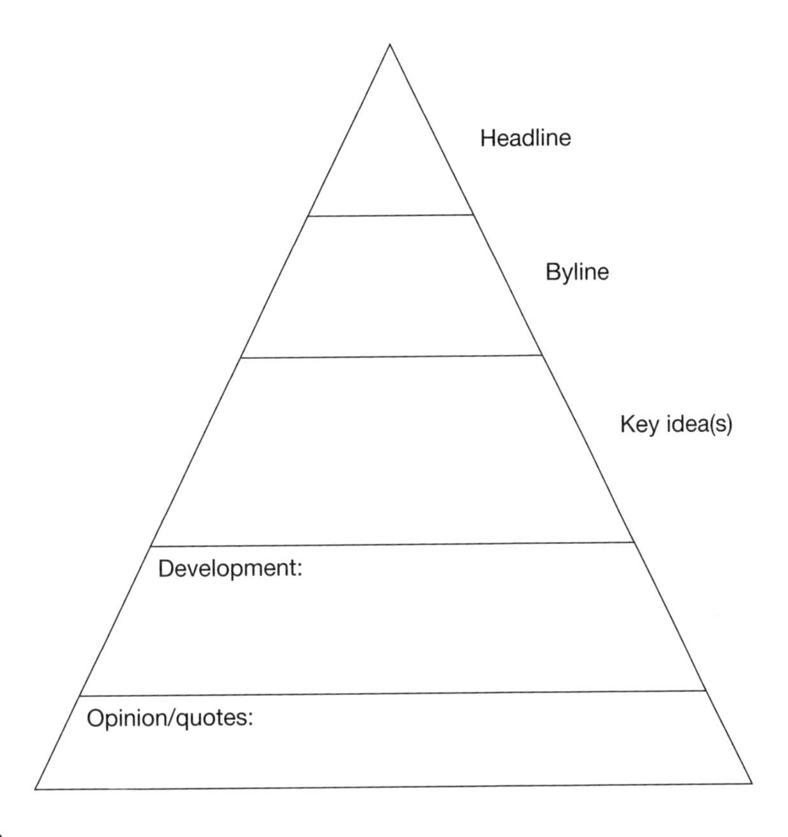

Figure 10

Notes:

- **Headline**. This needs to use a few 'strong' eye-catching words. It does not have to be a proper sentence.
- **Byline**. This is a proper sentence (or two) that tells the reader basically what the story is about.
- **Key idea(s)**. Or key events. This section recounts the main events of the story. Usually one short paragraph is used for each event or idea.
- **Development**. This is where you can go into more detail about the events or write about the background to the story.
- **Opinion/quotes**. Here you'll find comments by people linked to the events of the story. Sometimes there is a commentary stating the attitude or opinion of the newspaper.

(Tip: draw the pyramid template on to a sheet of A3 paper. Write your article in the different spaces in the pyramid. The reason for this is that you have to choose your words carefully, stick to the point and be brief.)

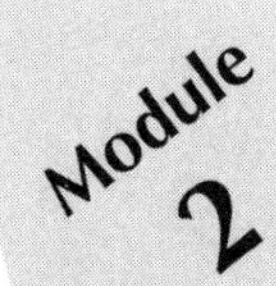

FOR THE PUPIL

Writing a letter

(There are no teacher's notes for this module.)

There is still a lot of debate among adults – teachers and parents included – about the importance of spelling, punctuation and grammar. Some adults believe that 'standards are dropping' in schools. (This may be a topic for a debate or written argument – see **Module 15** and counting down from there.) My own beliefs are:

- Spelling, punctuation and grammar are not so important when you're having your ideas, making notes and scribbling down your early thoughts.
- Spelling, punctuation and grammar are much more important when you 'make your work public'. That means showing the finished version to anyone else. 'Making public' is linked with the word 'publish', as you've probably guessed.

The point is that work you make public *represents you*. It says something about your standards and what you value. It speaks for you. For me anyway, because I care about what people think of my work, I take care over how I present it.

Of course it takes effort and concentration to do this, but there will come a time when that'll pay off . . .

My father-in-law worked in industry. He was in charge of a chemical lab for a big oil and petrol company. Very expensive and sometimes dangerous experiments were done in that lab.

Sometimes a job vacancy would come up and, once it was advertised, there'd be scores of applications, mostly from people who'd been to university. As the application letters came in, my father-in-law would say to his secretary:

> 'Jean, if any of the envelopes are not addressed properly, put them aside. Open the ones that are left. Those letters that aren't spelt and punctuated properly, put them aside. Of those that are left, read them through and if the sentences aren't clear, straightforward and accurate . . .'
>
> 'I know, put them aside,' said Jean.
>
> 'Yes. The small number that are left can be handed to me and I'll decide who I ask for interview.'
>
> 'But Des,' Jean said, 'you might be passing up some really talented people.'

'Maybe,' Des told her, 'but if they can't be bothered to take care over a letter, they probably won't be bothered to take care in my lab. And that's not acceptable.'

It's a story I've never forgotten, and one that perhaps you might think about.

You'll realise that the kind of letter I've been talking about is the more formal, 'official' business kind of letter. When you want to write one, here are some tips:

- Ask yourself (1) why am I writing this? and (2) what do I want to get out of it?
- What information does the letter need to contain?
- Be clear, straightforward and as brief as possible (good news – less writing to do!).
- Get the tone right . . .
  - Don't let your feelings get the better of you. Don't be offensive.
  - Don't try to be clever, sarcastic etc.
  - Be firm in stating your point/case or asking your question, but there's no need to be unfriendly. Politeness goes a long way.
- In your first paragraph state the main point of the letter.
- Make further points/develop your argument or case/build up to a request in the following paragraphs.
- Your final paragraph returns to the main point of the letter.
- I always end by thanking people for taking time to read my letter. Some folks don't put this in.
- Sign off. If you don't know the name of the person you're writing to, sign off 'Yours faithfully'. If you do know the reader's name, sign off 'Yours sincerely'. Some people advise you to put your initials and last name if you use 'Yours faithfully', and your first name and last name if you sign off 'Yours sincerely'.

The way the letter is set out on the page is also important. People's opinions vary, but I set out my letters like the one over the page . . .

FOR THE PUPIL

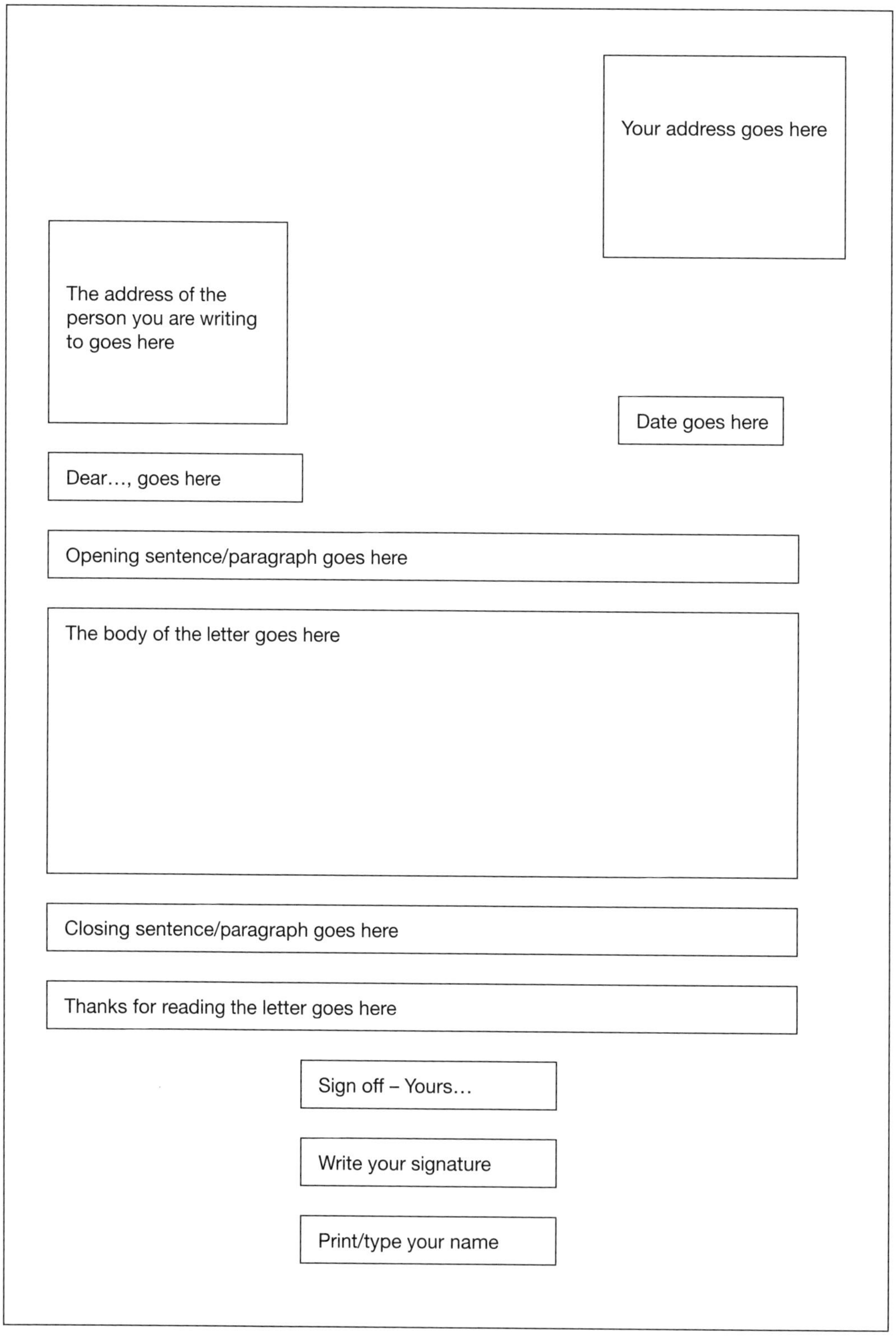
Your address goes here
The address of the person you are writing to goes here
Date goes here
Dear…, goes here
Opening sentence/paragraph goes here
The body of the letter goes here
Closing sentence/paragraph goes here
Thanks for reading the letter goes here
Sign off – Yours…
Write your signature
Print/type your name

Figure 11

Section 7 Putting it all together

A map of ideas

Concept mapping, similar to the mind mapping technique developed by Edward de Bono, is a visual organisation of ideas and the relationships between them. The main value of arranging information visually is that all of the material is available at a glance and is thus assimilated in its entirety, but connections can also be made and appreciated in the linear rational way of thinking, which is more the province of the 'left side of the brain' (very simplistically speaking).

Several visual organisers have been suggested throughout this book. Their use in a variety of contexts will help children to think more effectively and develop their creativity. There is not scope here to do more than touch upon the huge subject of concept mapping: if you want to learn more I recommend *Thinking Skills and Eye Q* by Oliver Caviglioli, Ian Harris and Bill Tindall, and Mel Rockett and Simon Percival's *Thinking for Learning* (see Bibliography).

Visual organisers also offer children a powerful and easy-to-use method of making notes, recording ideas in a way that is often more useful than the line-by-line method, which to me seems so cumbersome by comparison. Three very simple but flexible techniques are:

- overlapping circles
- continuum
- quadrant.

Overlapping circles

These are circles of various sizes arranged to suggest connections between ideas. The size of a circle can represent the importance of an idea or its complexity. The degree of overlap of circles indicates how closely ideas are related.

This technique can be done on paper but cutting out circles takes time (and it's boring!). The activity works much better using a computer, using the AutoShapes facility in a Word document, for instance. Text can be added and clipart or other pictures imported into the circles as required.

Examples of how the circle technique can be used include:

- Events happening at a certain time and place. Different-sized circles represent aspects of the event or contain notes from different witnesses/participants. Useful as preparatory work for a newspaper article.
- Points for and against a proposition in an argument. Circles can be colour coded for fact and opinion and their size will represent the relevance of the point to the issue in question. It's interesting to compare the size of circles containing the same point between different groups of children. Asking them to talk about why they gave circles certain sizes helps children to explore the argument further, as well as creating the opportunity for them to reflect on their values and beliefs.
- Use the circles to note the design features of an advertisement – how important each feature is to the impact of the finished product, and how the features influence each other.
- Personality profile. Draw a large circle to represent the whole person. Other smaller circles stand for feelings, attitudes, influences etc. Circles that lie partly outside the main one represent visible effects. So, for instance, if a red circle standing for anger overlapped the main circle it means that person lets his temper show. If the anger circle is entirely within the main one it indicates suppressed rage (but better out than in, I say).

Continuum

This is a simple linear organiser. It can be used as a story-planning device – see *Countdown to Creative Writing*, **Narrative lines** (**Module 38**) – or in other ways that are more applicable to non-fiction writing, for example:

- Pieces of information are arranged along the line from least to most important in preparation for a debate/argumentative essay.
- Children's names written on PostIt notes are arranged along the line depending on how strongly any child agrees/disagrees with a proposition. As a discussion develops some children may want to move their nametag as their view changes, perhaps writing their reason for the change on the tag.
- Use as a sequencing line for achieving a goal. Rank tasks in to-do order along the line, placing them at different heights to indicate their difficulty.

Quadrant

Use the template in Figure 12 in various ways:

- Facts and opinions for and against a proposition.
- Notes when evaluating information using the CARR plan – how current, accurate, reliable, relevant?
- As an extension of the 'three perceptual positions' (3PP) technique (see **Module 10**). The perceptual positions in this case would be individuals or groups for/against/neutral observer/undecided. Arrange chairs to reproduce the quadrant with a standing space in the middle. Different speakers for and against a proposition are invited to stand in the middle and offer a fact, opinion, argument etc. Children can move from one area of the quadrant to another if they change their mind. Children can also opt to become neutral observers if they want to 'detach' from their feelings in the matter and overview the argument more coolly.

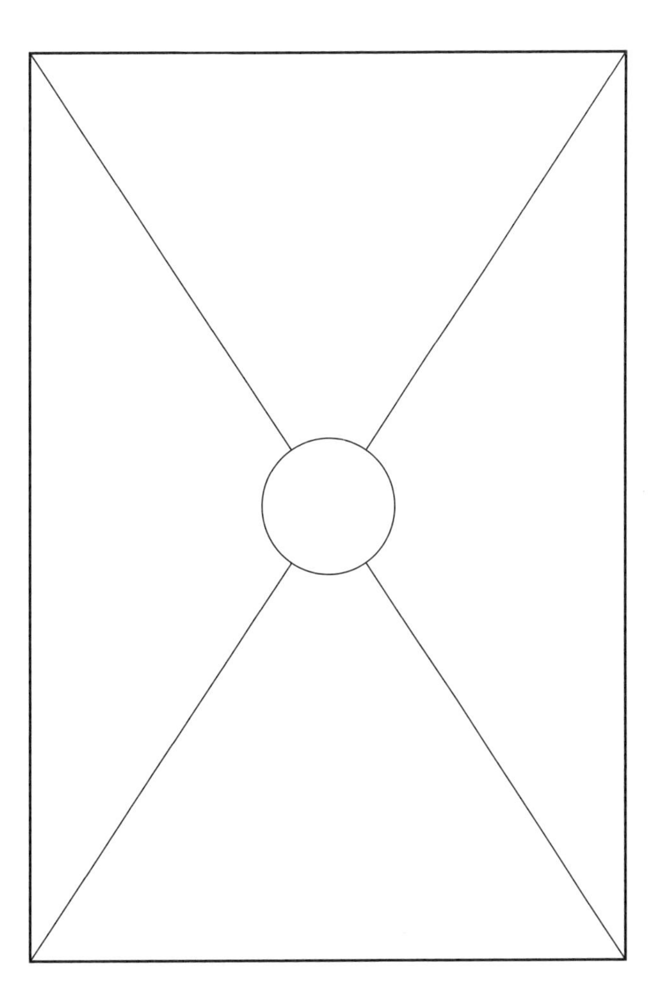

Figure 12

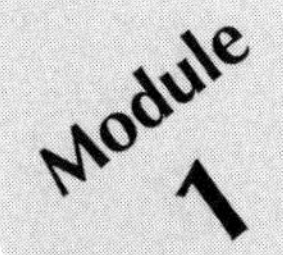

I'm sure you – and the children – will think of many other applications for these and other visual organisers. A useful resource for using them in the context of note-making is teacher and author Jim Burke's excellent website – www.englishcompanion.com/.

Be sure to check out the page – www.englishcompanion.com/Tools/notemaking.html.

FOR THE PUPIL

Module 1

A map of ideas

The good news is that I'm not going to say very much in this module! The even better news is that your teacher might want you to try out some games about how you can arrange ideas you have.

Well, that's just about it. We're almost at the end of the book. I hope you've learned some useful things about language and feelings, facts and truth and opinions. A writer called Henry Brooke Adams once said that 'words are slippery but language is viscous.' ('Viscous' means thick like mud). Perhaps now you're better able to hold on to those slippery words long enough to see what they're up to.

But enough from me – I think you might be ready to BLASTOFF!

Review

Language helps to make us what we are. We all own language, it is nobody's special property. It is a wonderful friend but can be a terrible enemy. I hope this book has helped you to own language and not let language own you. To make sure of this, remember:

- 'Question, doubt, challenge'.
- CARR – is the information current, accurate, reliable, relevant?
- Style, purpose, audience.

And sometimes, as the writer Robert Benchley advised us . . .

Drawing on my great command of the language, I chose to say nothing.

Bibliography

Abbot, John (with MacTaggart, Heather) (2009) *Overschooled but Undereducated.* London: Network Continuum Education.

Abbot, John and Ryan, Terry (2000) *The Unfinished Revolution*. Stafford: Network Educational Press.

Bloom, Benjamin (1958) *The Taxonomy of Educational Objectives*. London: Longman.

Bowkett, Steve (1999) *Catch & Other Stories.* Bewdley: Crazy Horse Press.

Bowkett, Steve (2001) *ALPS StoryMaker: Using fiction as a resource for accelerated learning*. Stafford: Network Educational Press.

Bowkett, Steve (2007) *Jumpstart! Creativity*. London and New York: Routledge.

Bowkett, Steve (2007) *100+ Ideas for Teaching Thinking Skills/100+ Ideas for Teaching Creativity*. London: Network Continuum.

Bowkett, Steve (2009) *Countdown to Creative Writing*. London and New York: Routledge.

Bryson, Bill (1991) *Mother Tongue*. London: Penguin Books.

Caviglioli, Oliver, Harris, Ian and Tindall, Bill (2004) *Thinking Skills & Eye Q*. London: Network Continuum.

Czerneda, Julie (1999) *No Limits: Developing scientific literacy using science fiction*. Toronto: Trifolium Books.

Freebody, Peter and Luke, Allan (1990) Literacies programs: debates and demands in cultural context. *Prospect: Australian Journal of TESOL*, 5(7): 7–16.

Humphrys, John (2004) *Lost for Words: The mangling and manipulating of the English language*. London: Hodder & Stoughton.

Law, Stephen (2000/2003) *The Philosophy Files 1 & 2*. London: Orion.

Leech, Geoffrey (1966) *English in Advertising: A linguistic study of advertising in Great Britain*. London: Longman.

Morgan, Norah and Saxton, Juliana (1994) *Asking Better Questions*. Markham, ONT: Pembroke.

O'Connor, Joseph and Seymour, John (1990) *Introducing Neuro-Linguistic Programming*. London: Mandala (HarperCollins).

Postman, Neil and Weingartner, Charles (1971) *Teaching as a Subversive Activity*. Harmondsworth: Penguin Education Specials.

Rockett, Mel and Percival, Simon (2002) *Thinking for Learning*. Stafford: Network Educational Press.

Schrank, Jeffrey (1996) The language of advertising claims, *Handouts, English 102*. Oxford, MS: University of Mississippi.

Slater, Don (1984) *Wok Cookery*. Ware: Omega Books. (If you are at all interested in Chinese cookery I heartily recommend this book. It's a brilliantly useful instructional manual laced with humour and 'gustatory' language. Last time I looked, used copies were available on Amazon.)

Stanley, Sara (with Bowkett, Steve) (2004) *But Why? Developing philosophical thinking in the classroom*. Stafford: Network Educational Press (now Network Continuum).

Strunk, William and White, Elwyn Brooks (2000) *The Elements of Style*, 4th edition. New York: Longman.

van den Brink-Budgen, Roy (2004) *Critical Thinking for Students*, 3rd edition. Oxford: How to Books.

Watson, Don (2005) *Gobbledygook: How clichés, sludge and management-speak are strangling our public language*. London: Atlantic Books.

Index

Numbers refer to Module numbers. **Bold** numbers indicate that the topic appears also in the **Teacher's Notes**. Asterisks (*) indicate extension material is available on the website.